Reason To *Write*

Strategies for Success in Academic Writing

HIGH BEGINNING

Judy L. Miller
and
Robert F. Cohen

OXFORD
UNIVERSITY PRESS

OXFORD
UNIVERSITY PRESS
198 Madison Avenue
New York, NY 10016 USA
Great Clarendon Street, Oxford OX2 6DP UK

Oxford University Press is a department of the University of Oxford.
It furthers the University's objective of excellence in research,
scholarship, and education by publishing worldwide in

Oxford   New York

Auckland   Cape Town   Dar es Salaam   Hong Kong   Karachi   Kuala
Lumpur   Madrid   Melbourne   Mexico City   Nairobi   New Delhi
Shanghai   Taipei   Toronto

With offices in

Argentina   Austria   Brazil   Chile   Czech Republic   France   Greece
Guatemala   Hungary   Italy   Japan   Poland   Portugal   Singapore
South Korea   Switzerland   Thailand   Turkey   Ukraine   Vietnam

OXFORD and OXFORD ENGLISH are registered trademarks of Oxford
University Press.

© Oxford University Press 2006

Database right Oxford University Press (maker)

Library of Congress Cataloging-in-Publication Data

Miller, Judy L., 1947–
    Reason to write, high beginning: strategies for success in
academic writing / Judy L. Miller, Robert F. Cohen.
        p. cm.
    ISBN-13: 978-0-19-431120-5 (pbk.)
    ISBN-10: 0-19-431120-1 (pbk.)
    1. English language—Rhetoric—Problems, exercises, etc. 2.
English language—Textbooks for foreign speakers. 3. Academic
writing—Problems, exercises, etc. I. Cohen, Robert F., 1946– II.
Title.

PE1413.M553 2005
808'.0428—dc22   2005018035

Editorial Manager: Janet Aitchison
Senior Acquisitions Editor: Pietro Alongi
Editor: Dena Daniel
Associate Editor: Scott Allan Wallick
Art Director: Maj-Britt Hagsted
Senior Designer: Michael Steinhofer
Art Editor: Judi DeSouter
Production Manager: Shanta Persaud
Production Controller: Zai Jawat Ali

ISBN-13: 978 0 19 431120 5
ISBN-10: 0 19 431120 1

Printed in Hong Kong

10 9 8 7 6 5 4 3 2 1

ACKNOWLEDGMENTS

Illustrations: Vilma Ortiz Dillon: 50, 73; Karen Minot: 1, 62, 68, 69,
70; Peanuts © United Feature Syndicate, Inc.: 13

*The publishers would like to thank the following for their permission to
reproduce photographs:*

Punchstock: Comstock, 1, Dynamic Graphics, 66; Getty Images:
Getty Images News, 20, Lewis W. Hine, 37, 44, Mark
Cremer/Iconica, 49; Brian Sahd/New York Restoration Project: 25;
Workbook.com: eStock Photo, 49, Greg Friedler, 85; Grant Heilman
Photography, Inc.: 54; Magnum Photos/Richard Kalvar: 61

The publishers would also like to thank the following for their help:

"Equal Inheritance," "The King and the Shirt," from *Fables and Fairy
Tales* by Leo Tolstoy, translated by Ann Dunnigan, copyright © 1962
by Ann Dunnigan. Used by permission of Dutton Signet, a division
of Penguin Group (USA) Inc.

Excerpt from *The Namesake* by Jhumpa Lahiri. Copyright © 2003 by
Jhumpa Lahiri. Adapted and reprinted by permission of Houghton
Mifflin Company. All rights reserved.

Excerpt from *The Full Cupboard of Life* by Alexander McCall Smith.
Copyright © 2003 by Alexander McCall Smith. Published by
Pantheon Books, a division of Random House, Inc.

"Growth of Literacy Rates" graph and "Literacy in Latin America
and the Caribbean" graph from "50 Years for Education and
Society." Adapted and reprinted by permission of UNESCO.

Author Acknowledgements

Heartfelt and grateful thanks go to our editor Amy Cooper. Her intelligence, creativity, and care have guided us in all our work. We thank Amy not only for her professionalism but also for the gift of her friendship. We are grateful to Pietro Alongi for the insight and efficiency he has brought to this project from beginning to end. We also thank Janet Aitchison for her support and encouragement in the conception of this series.

Our sincere thanks also go to Carla Mavrodin, Dena Daniel, Scott Allan Wallick, Maj-Britt Hagsted, and Judi DeSouter for their essential contributions to this project.

We thank our colleagues at the American Language Program at Columbia University and the Department of Language and Cognition at Eugenio Maria de Hostos Community College for their professional support and good will.

Finally, we remember our students, from whom we continue to learn every day and who remain in our hearts our true teachers.

With love to Nora, Ernest, Max, and Daniel.

Judy L. Miller

With love to my mother, Lillian Kumock Cohen, and the whole family tree.

Robert F. Cohen

REASON TO WRITE

STRATEGIES FOR SUCCESS IN ACADEMIC WRITING

Introduction to the Series

Writing in one's own language is difficult enough. Imagine how much more daunting a task it is for students to write in a second language. If the weight of writer's block does not inhibit their impulse to move forward with a writing assignment, their insecurity with the language and its particular writing culture sometimes makes them stare at the blank page with trepidation. Writing teachers thus have a dual challenge: Not only must they help the most reticent and timid writers overcome a potentially crippling writing phobia, but they must also instill in their students the confidence needed to translate their thoughts into correct and acceptable English. The communicative approach that we use in the *Reason To Write* series will help teachers to achieve this end.

Even though the writing product is an expression of one's individuality and personality, it is important to remember that writing is also a social endeavor, a way of communicating with others, informing them, persuading them, and debating with them. In our attempt to provide guidelines, strategies, and practice in writing for university, community college, and high school students preparing for the academic demands of all disciplines in higher education, we want students to realize that they are not writing in a vacuum. They have a voice, and what they write will elicit a reaction from others. In our books writing is, therefore, an active communicative/social process involving discussion, interaction with teachers, group work, pair work, and peer evaluation. Through these collaborative experiences, students come to recognize their unique strengths while they cultivate their critical thinking skills and become more effective writers.

Content-based themes that speak to both the hearts and minds of students are the key to realizing our goal. Writing can develop only where there is meaning; it cannot be an empty exercise in form. And meaning cannot be understood unless students are given intellectually challenging and emotionally appealing material that generates their enthusiasm. Because all instruction in grammar, vocabulary, and rhetorical styles is presented in relation to a theme, each unit provides a seamless path from reading to thinking to writing, from the preparatory stages of writing to the completion of a final written composition. Working with one theme, the whole class experiences the same problem or issue at the same time, and students benefit from the security of the shared discussion and exploration. As a result, writers are not left to suffer alone with the blank page. At the same time, students are given several writing options within each theme so that there is ample opportunity for individual expression.

Content-based themes also encourage the kind of critical thinking that students are expected to do across the curriculum in a college or university. Because many students may lack some of the analytical skills needed to do academic work, we provide them with experience in analyzing ideas, making inferences, supporting opinions, understanding points of view, and writing for different audiences. As students "reason to write," they practice the skills and strategies that are vital for academic success, and they have an opportunity to write on a wide variety of themes that reflect the academic curriculum.

The High Beginner Book

This book is intended for students who have probably had more opportunities to speak the language than to write it. As a result, formal writing conventions and requirements may be unfamiliar to them. This book is designed to provide simple yet meaningful writing tasks that will build confidence and competence in an academic context.

In this book, there are four main sections in each unit.

I. Thinking About the Topic

All units in this book begin with a simple unstructured writing activity that can be limited to composing a list, formulating a question, expressing a preference, or detailing an observation. Students can freely express their thoughts and share them with a partner, without worrying about grammar or spelling. Students explore the theme of the unit by drawing on their own knowledge and ideas. As a result, they enter the subsequent discussions with more self-assurance.

II. Reading for Writing

In order to develop as a writer, one must be a reader. Therefore, each unit contains a short provocative reading passage, usually one or two paragraphs long, followed by a series of discussion activities and simple writing exercises. In this section, students consider readings that deal with a variety of topics: names and family, the role of nature, homelessness, freedom, happiness, literacy, child labor, and video games. They do so by answering questions that first test their literal comprehension skills and then summon their ability to think inferentially. Through the discussion questions provided, students are encouraged to begin to formulate and then express their opinions in writing, a process that will culminate in the main writing task of the unit.

III. Writing Focus

If the Reading for Writing section aims to convince students that they have something to say about significant themes, the Writing Focus section provides them with additional tools to express their contribution effectively. This section is divided into three parts, Language for Writing, Words and Ideas, and Your Task (the main writing assignment).

In Language for Writing, students practice the grammar point they must master in order to embark on the writing task. They practice using the simple present tense, *should*, the *will* future tense, the simple past tense, comparative forms such as *more than/fewer than/less than*, verbs such as *want, would like*, and *ask*, and gerunds and infinitives.

In Words and Ideas, students develop various lexical skills as they expand their vocabulary and learn different word forms. They practice working with adjectives, adverbs of manner, prefixes, prepositions and prepositional phrases, words that explain data, noun and adjective word forms, and expressions of opinion. As students strive to achieve competency in these sections, they continue to address the theme of the unit in greater depth. They learn to take ownership of their point of view. Students give and receive immediate feedback through ongoing dialogue with a partner or a group, developing ideas and building confidence for the main writing task.

In Your Task, students are given step-by-step guidance through the writing process. Because we feel that students should be given choices, we provide a writing task and an alternative task; both are specifically prepared in the unit. The writing task evolves from sentence-level writing in the early units to writing paragraphs by the end of the book. To give students the support they need to accomplish the writing task, we provide a model for them to follow. The model is on a topic similar to the writing topics.

From Step 1 (Getting Ideas) through Step 4 (Revising), students work on a first draft after brainstorming, organizing their ideas, examining models, and learning certain essential rules of rhetoric. In Step 4, when students finally read their sentences or paragraph to a partner, they are given the opportunity to decide whether or not they need to modify the content in any way. Through such sharing, peer evaluation becomes an integral part of the writing process. The class becomes a "writing workshop" in which the writing process is demystified and students learn how to look critically at their own work. Our guidelines for peer work ensure that this is a positive experience, a prelude but not a substitute for feedback from the teacher. In Step 5 (Editing), students learn yet another grammar point or rule of punctuation they will need to bring the writing assignment to fruition. They are given practice with this new point before they are asked in a Checklist for Editing to proofread their own work. The information that was taught in both the Language for Writing and Editing sections of the unit is highlighted here.

In this beginning book of the series, students go from writing complete sentences to connecting these sentences in small paragraphs. They learn the rudiments of writing a well-developed paragraph. They learn how to organize a coherent paragraph as they practice writing topic sentences and concluding sentences and providing the necessary support for these statements. They learn to perfect these skills by performing tasks as varied as explaining their name, writing a letter of advice, writing a formal letter, writing a narrative paragraph, writing a descriptive paragraph, writing a paragraph to explain a graph, writing an analysis of a short story, and writing an opinion paragraph. In the end, when they have completed the last unit, the process of formulating ideas, communicating them in sentences, and weaving them into paragraphs has become clear.

IV. Additional Writing Opportunities

In this section students are given the opportunity to write on a wide variety of additional simple topics inspired by the reading. They also have the opportunity to do Internet research and write journal responses. As students avail themselves of the additional writing practice in each unit, they will come that much closer to developing the skills and confidence they need to become independent writers.

In conclusion, the *Reason to Write* series represents our effort to integrate the insights of whole language learning and writing workshops across the curriculum at the college level. These books were also written with the knowledge that no textbook can come to life and be effective without the creative contributions of the teachers and students who use it. We hope that you and your students will develop a strong connection with the material in this book and thus form a bond with us as you explore the writing process. We would appreciate any suggestions or comments you may have. You can write to us in care of Oxford University Press, ESL Department, 198 Madison Avenue, New York, New York 10016-4314.

Judy L. Miller and Robert F. Cohen

CONTENTS

The Most Popular Baby Names in the U.S.

BOYS	GIRLS
Jacob	Emily
Aidan	Emma
Ethan	Madison
Matthew	Hanna
Nicholas	Hailey
Joshua	Sarah
Ryan	Kaitlyn
Michael	Isabella
Zachary	Olivia
Tyler	Abigail

WRITING ABOUT YOUR NAME

In this unit you will practice:
- writing complete sentences
- using the simple present tense
- working with adjectives
- using capital letters correctly

I Thinking About the Topic

Look at the lists of names above. Then think about these questions. Discuss your answers in small groups.

Do you think a name is important? Why or why not? Which names in the lists do you like best? What are some popular names for boys and girls among your family members and friends?

In your groups, write a list of the popular names you discussed. Share your lists with the class.

Reading for Writing

In this reading, adapted from *The Namesake* by Jhumpa Lahiri, Ashima and her husband Ashoke have a newborn baby boy. He was born in the United States. This conversation takes place in the hospital a few days after the baby's birth.

Ashima and Ashoke learn that in America a baby cannot leave the hospital without a name.

"But sir," Ashima protests, "we can't name him ourselves."

Mr. Wilcox looks at the hospital birth certificate and looks at the couple.
5 He looks at the nameless child. "I see," he says. "Why?"

"We are waiting for a letter from my grandmother in India," says Ashima. "She will name the baby. She gives the names for all her great-grandchildren."

The letter with the name is late. Ashima and Ashoke are not worried.
10 They can wait. In India, parents take their time, even years, to find the right name. Besides, there are always pet names. A pet name is the name your family and friends call you. A Bengali[1] usually has both a pet name and a good name for use in the outside world.

"You can name him after yourself or one of your ancestors,"[2] said Mr.
15 Wilcox. "It's a fine tradition."

But this is not possible, Ashima and Ashoke think to themselves. This tradition—naming a child after a parent or grandparent—is a sign of respect[3] in America and Europe, but it doesn't exist for Bengalis. In Bengali families, individual names are sacred.[4] Bengalis cannot inherit[5] or
20 share names.

Mr. Wilcox sighs. "You can name him 'Baby Boy' for now, but when he gets his name, you must go to a judge and pay money to change the birth certificate. Think about it, I'll be back in a few hours."

---

1. *Bengali*: (n.) a person from Bengal, a place that is now partly in India and partly in Bangladesh; (adj.) from or connected with Bengal
2. *ancestor*: a family member who lived a long time ago
3. *respect*: a feeling that you admire or have a high opinion of someone
4. *sacred*: very special; very important to someone
5. *inherit*: receive something from someone who died

General Understanding

1. Comparing Cultures

Fill in the chart with information from the reading. Compare answers with a partner.

	United States culture	Bengali culture
1. Who usually chooses a child's name?	the parents	
2. When does a child get a name?		
3. Can people name their child after another family member?		

2. Explaining Reasons

Complete these sentences. Compare answers with a partner.

1. Ashima and Ashoke have a problem because they _____

   _____

   _____

2. The parents cannot name this baby because they _____

   _____

   _____

3. The baby cannot leave the hospital because he _____

   _____

   _____

4. Bengali parents cannot name a child after another family member because each name _____

   _____

   _____

3. Your Turn

How do you think Ashima and Ashoke's story will end? Write your answer. Then take turns reading your responses in small groups.

_____

_____

_____

4. Open for Discussion

Think about these questions. Discuss your answers in small groups.

1. Do you think Mr. Wilcox understands Ashima and Ashoke? Why or why not?

2. Why do you think Ashima and Ashoke want their grandparent to choose the child's name?

3. Why do you think Americans name their children very quickly? What happens to a baby without a name?

4. Who chooses names in your family? Is there a special naming celebration? Compare your family's traditions with Bengali traditions.

After your discussions, choose one question and write your answer. Remember to write complete sentences.

_____

_____

_____

_____

III ▸ Writing Focus

A. Language for Writing: The Simple Present Tense

1. Use the simple present to write about:

• A regular activity or habit	**A baby often cries.**
• Thoughts or feelings	**I like my nickname.**
• A general fact	**Bengalis don't share names.**

2. To form the simple present of **regular verbs**, use the base form of the verb. With *he, she, it* or a singular noun*, add *-s* to the base form. To form negative statements, use *do/does* + *not* before the base form.

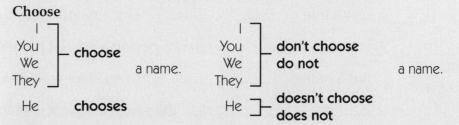

Choose

| I You We They | **choose** | a name. |
| He | **chooses** | |

| I You We They | **don't choose** **do not** | a name. |
| He | **doesn't choose** **does not** | |

Have and *be* are **irregular verbs**.

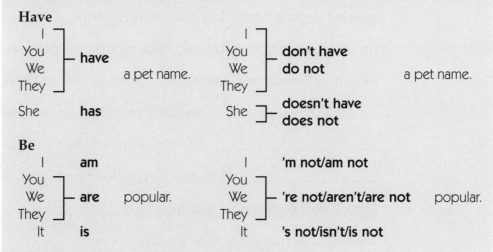

Have

| I You We They | **have** | a pet name. |
| She | **has** | |

| I You We They | **don't have** **do not** | a pet name. |
| She | **doesn't have** **does not** | |

Be

I	**am**	
You We They	**are**	popular.
It	**is**	

I	**'m not/am not**	
You We They	**'re not/aren't/are not**	popular.
It	**'s not/isn't/is not**	

*Spelling notes for third person singular forms:

- When the base form ends with a consonant before *-y*, change *-y* to *-ies*:

  You **try**   He **tries**

- When there is a vowel before the *-y*, add only *–s*:

  I **play**   She **plays**

1. Working on the Simple Present Tense

Correct the errors in these sentences. Compare answers with a partner.

1. The grandmother ~~give~~ *gives* the baby a name.

2. A baby crys for many reasons.

3. Ashoke hasn't an English name.

4. Ashima no is comfortable with American naming traditions.

5. Who pay for a name change?

2. Completing a Paragraph

Fill in the blanks in the paragraph. Use the simple present forms of the verbs in parentheses. Compare answers with a partner.

A name _____is_____ (be) a wonderful thing because it
                    1

_____ (give) a person a special place in the world.
          2

But a name _____ (not/stop) with one person. It
                      3

_____ (tell) the story of a person's family and the
          4

many people who _____ (be) a part of the family's
                          5

present or past. Many last names in English _____
                                                          6

(have) interesting histories. For example, some names come from

jobs, like Farmer or Cook. Others, such as Hill or Bush,

_____ (be) words from nature. A name ending in
          7

son _____ (come) from a father's name. Peterson
              8

_____ (mean) son of Peter and Johnson means son of
          9

John. Color or physical qualities also _____ (explain)
                                                    10

the origin of names such as Brown or Long.

B. Words and Ideas: Adjectives

An **adjective** describes a person, place, or thing.

1. You can use adjectives before a noun.

   An **honest** person always tells the truth.

2. You can also use adjectives after verbs such as *be* or *seem*.

   Fatima is **honest**. She never tells a lie.
   Paulo seems **hardworking**. He spends hours on his homework.

1. The Meaning of Names

Read the names and descriptions of the people. Which people have names that describe their personalities?

CATHERINE means "perfect."

Catherine is an <u>attractive</u> person. People like her because she is pretty and she has a pleasant personality.

JESSICA means "wealthy."

Jessica is a <u>confident</u> person. She feels that she does many things well.

LUCY means "light."

Lucy is a <u>cheerful</u> person. She laughs easily and puts her friends in a good mood.

BEN means "son."

Ben is <u>shy</u>. He is nervous when he meets new people. He likes to stay home.

ROBERT means "famous."

Robert is an <u>athletic</u> person. He plays on many different sports teams and enjoys exercise.

JAMAL means "handsome."

Jamal is <u>talkative</u>. He always has something interesting to say.

2. Choosing Adjectives

Fill in the blanks in the sentences below with these adjectives. Use each adjective only once. Compare answers with a partner.

athletic	**attractive**	**cheerful**	**confident**
hardworking	**honest**	**shy**	**talkative**

1. Tae Yon always asks me questions and tells me lots of stories. She is a

   very _____talkative_____ person.

2. Carlos has many problems, but he tries to be happy and

   _____ with other people.

3. My brother is a _____ driver because he has a lot of

   experience on the road.

4. My friend Bob is on our school's basketball, soccer, and swimming

   teams. He's very _____.

5. Mario is good-looking and very _____ in his new suit.

6. Claudia has a job during the day and she goes to school at night. She is

   a _____ person.

7. Ilya is very timid, nervous, and _____ with strangers.

8. Gina never tells a lie. She is a very _____ person, and

   I trust her.

Write three sentences about yourself with the adjectives in the list above. Share your sentences with a partner.

_____

_____

_____

YOUR TASK

Write about your first name.
or
Write about your last name (family name).

Before you write, study steps 1–3 and the examples below.

Step 1:   Getting Ideas

Ask yourself the questions below. Write notes for your answers.
You may add other ideas.

1. What is your family name? _Cook_

2. Does the name have a meaning? _yes—someone who prepares food_

3. Do you like your name? _yes—easy to spell_

4. Do people remember it easily? _yes—simple_

Step 2:   Writing Sentences from Your Notes

Put your answers into complete sentences.

My name is Cook.

A cook prepares food.

I like my name because it is easy to spell.

People remember my name because it is simple.

Step 3:   Writing Sentences in a Paragraph

Write the sentences all together in a paragraph. Add two more ideas. Give the paragraph a title.

My Family Name

   My last name is Cook. A cook prepares food. I like my name because it is easy to spell in English. Cook is a simple name, and people remember it. The people in my family are hardworking and honest. I think about my family and our name, and I feel more confident.

What's in a Name?

Now follow the steps below to write your paragraph.

Step 1: Answer the questions below. Then choose two or three questions to write about. You may add other ideas.

1. What is your first name? _____

2. What does it mean? _____

3. Do you like your name? Why or why not? _____

_____

4. Do you have a nickname or pet name? What is it? Do you like it?

_____

5. Does your name describe your personality? What adjectives describe

   you well? _____

_____

Step 2: Put your answers into complete sentences.
Step 3: Write your sentences all together in a paragraph.
Step 4: Revising

Work with a partner. Read each other's paragraphs, and write comments in the margin. Use the checklist below and see the example on page 11. Don't worry about grammar errors.

CHECKLIST FOR REVISING

1. Write a check (✓) next to the sentence or idea you like best.

2. Write a question mark (?) next to any part of the writing that is not clear to you.

Review your paragraph. Do you want to change any part of your writing to make it clearer? Do you want to add other ideas?

Step 5:   Editing—Capital Letters

Use **capital letters** for names of countries, nationalities, and languages.

Countries: France, Mexico, China, Russia, the United States, the Dominican Republic

Nationalities: French, Mexican, Chinese, Russian, American, Dominican

Languages: French, Spanish, Chinese, Russian, English

There are 10 errors of capitalization in this paragraph. The first one is corrected for you. Find 9 more errors and correct them.

     United States

In the ~~united States~~, there are many last names from other languages.

There are polish names like Polanski, chinese names like Woo, Italian

names like pacino, korean names like Park, and spanish names like Lopez.

Some names can be written in Greek or arabic letters. A family name such

as Pavlova means "a female member of the pavlov family" in russian. All

these names tell the story of america.

Read each sentence of your paragraph carefully. Edit any grammar errors you find. Use the checklist below.

> ## CHECKLIST FOR EDITING
>
> 1. **Did you add -s to the simple present verbs with *he, she,* or *it* as the subject?**
>
> 2. **Did you capitalize the names of countries, nationalities, and languages?**

 # *IV* Additional Writing Opportunities

Choose one of the following topics and write a response of at least two or three sentences.

1. Many women take their husband's last name when they get married. Men: Do you want your wife to take your name when you get married? Women: Do you want to change your name when you get married? Explain your answer.

2. Do you think a name is important? Why or why not?

3. Write a short paragraph with the title: What I Like About Myself.

4. INTERNET RESEARCH: Think of a country. What is the origin of the country's name? What does it mean? Is there an English form of the country's name? What is it? What is the origin of the English name? Search for the information on the Internet and prepare a short report for your class.

 ### Journal Writing

It is helpful to keep a journal in English. Write in your journal at least once a week. Keeping a journal will help you feel comfortable writing in English.

In your journal, write a response to the following questions. Try to express yourself as well as you can. Don't worry about mistakes. Try to write half a page.

What kind of personality do you have? What are the people in your family like? Describe yourself and your family members.

2 GIVING ADVICE

Peanuts: © United Feature Syndicate, Inc

WRITING A LETTER OF ADVICE

In this unit you will practice:
- giving advice and stating reasons
- using *should*
- using adjectives ending in *-ing* and *-ed*
- fixing comma splices

 Thinking About the Topic

Look at the cartoon. Then think about these questions. Discuss your answers in small groups.

What is happening in this cartoon?
Why is it funny?
Who do you usually ask for advice?
Do people ask you for advice? When?

II ▸ Reading for Writing

SOUTHSIDE CITY GAZETTE
READERS' FORUM

Dear Gazette Readers,

I need your advice. Here's the situation. Every day on my way to school, I see a man on the street. He always asks for money. He looks like a homeless person. Should I give money to people on the street? How much money should I give? I don't know what to do.

Confused

Letter 1
Dear Confused,

I feel sorry for people who ask for money on the street. Many people want to work, but there is a lot of unemployment. Sometimes they cannot find a job, and they get depressed.

Also, many people are homeless, and they have no family to help them. Housing is very expensive now. In addition, many people are cold and hungry. I think about each situation and decide what to do. Sometimes I give a little money or some food. In the winter, I sometimes give a hat or gloves. We should try to help.

Helping Out

Letter 2
Dear Confused,

You should not give money to people on the street. I have two reasons for this advice.

First of all, everyone has to earn money. This man should get a job. Why should you give your money to him? Are you very rich?

Second, you shouldn't give money to people on the street because they usually don't spend your money on healthy things. Instead, you should give the money to an organization that helps homeless people.

A Neighbor

General Understanding

1. True or False?

Mark these statements T (true) or F (false). Compare answers with a partner.

_____ 1. "Confused" is asking advice about giving money.

_____ 2. "Helping Out" always gives money to street people.

_____ 3. "Helping Out" sometimes gives money to organizations that help the homeless.

_____ 4. "A Neighbor" thinks you should give money to street people.

2. Explaining Reasons

Work with a partner. Answer these questions. Put a check (✓) next to your answers. There is more than one correct answer for each question.

1. Which reasons does "Helping Out" give **for** giving money to people on the street?

_____ a. Housing costs a lot of money.

_____ b. There are many people out of work.

_____ c. Some people don't have to obey the rules.

_____ d. Sometimes giving money is helpful.

2. Which reasons does "A Neighbor" give **against** giving money to people on the street?

_____ a. It is important for people to work.

_____ b. People on the street are not really poor.

_____ c. People often waste the money you give them.

_____ d. There are better ways to help poor people.

3. Your Turn

Which of the letters do you agree with? Why? Write your answer. Then take turns reading your answers in small groups.

_____

_____

_____

_____

4. Open for Discussion

Do you agree or disagree with these statements? Why? Discuss your answers in small groups.

1. Homeless people don't want to work.

2. The government needs to provide homes for the homeless.

3. College students don't have time to help homeless people.

After your discussions, choose one statement and write what you think about it. Remember to write complete sentences.

_____

_____

_____

_____

III Writing Focus

A. Language for Writing: *Should* and *Shouldn't*

Use *should* to offer advice. *You should study hard* means "In my opinion, it is good for you to study hard."

1. **To form statements** use this pattern*:

		should +	base form of the verb	
You	**should**	**help**	homeless people.
You	**shouldn't**	**waste**	your money.

*Use the same pattern for all pronouns (*I, you, he/she/it, we, they*).

2. **To form questions** use this pattern:

		should +	subject +	base form of the verb	
	Should	you	**give**	money?
	Shouldn't	we	**try**	to help?
What	**should**	I		do?
	shouldn't			

1. Correcting Statements with *Should*

Work with a partner. Correct the errors in these sentences.

1. What should she gave?

   <u>What should she give?</u>

2. Should we to give our money to homeless people?

   _____

3. I should telling the police about the problem.

   _____

4. He shouldn't gives his money to homeless people.

   _____

5. What we should do?

   _____

2. Completing Sentences with *Should* and *Shouldn't*

Fill in the blanks in the letter with should *or* shouldn't *and the words in parentheses. Compare answers with a partner.*

Dear Gazette Readers,

So many people are homeless. What ___should we do___ (*we/do*)? First of all, the government _____ (*build*) more low-cost housing. Private builders _____ (*have*) this responsibility because they don't make enough money on low-cost housing. In addition, the government _____ (*raise*) the minimum wage to more than $8 an hour so that people can pay for their homes.

Most homeless people are women and children. Most of them do not ask for money. Children _____ (*live*) in shelters because it is bad for their health and education. They need a home. Also, we _____ (*create*) more centers for people with drug and alcohol problems. The United States is a strong country. _____ (*we/care*) more about our people? Everyone _____ (*have*) a home because privacy and a peaceful place to live are part of our basic human rights.

Sincerely,
Very Worried

B. Words and Ideas:
Adjectives Ending in *-ing* and *-ed*

Adjectives that end in *-ing* or *-ed* refer to feelings.

1. An adjective that ends in *-ing* describes a noun that causes a feeling.

   Homelessness is a **depressing** situation.

2. An adjective that ends in *-ed* describes a noun that has or experiences a feeling.

   Homeless people are often **depressed** about their lives.

1. Recognizing Meanings

Work with a partner. Fill in the blanks in the sentences below with these adjectives.

bored	**depressed**	**frightened**
interested	**surprised**	**thrilled**

1. I thought most homeless people were men. I was ___surprised___₁

   to learn that they are mainly women and children.

2. I am _____ in finding out more about the homeless problem.
   ₂

3. Without a home, a family can be very sad and _____ about
   ₃

   their lives.

4. Crowded homeless shelters are often scary places for children; they are

   _____ by all the people they don't know.
   ₄

5. Sometimes the children have nothing to do all day. They get

   _____.
   ₅

6. It's exciting for a family to finally get a home. They are always

   _____ to hear the news.
   ₆

2. Recognizing Word Forms

Fill in the blanks in the ad with the correct form of the adjectives. Compare answers with a partner.

TRY SOMETHING NEW!

Are you ___bored___ *(boring/bored)* with your usual

1

school vacations? Come join us! Work for Habitat for

Humanity and help homeless families. Your Spring Break

won't be _____ *(boring/bored)* anymore!

2

Be a volunteer worker and build houses that homeless

families can buy at low cost. It's _____

3

(interesting/interested) work and you'll get to meet hundreds of

young people like yourselves from all over the country. You'll

be _____ *(surprising/surprised)* how quickly the time

4

goes by.

Homelessness is a _____ *(frightening/frightened)*

5

experience for people. But you will see their smiles when they

get the _____ *(thrilling/thrilled)* news about a home.

6

Are you _____ *(depressing/depressed)* about

7

homelessness? Do something to help! Join Habitat for

Humanity! We have offices all over the world.

YOUR TASK

Choose one of the letters below and write a response for a neighborhood newspaper. Give your advice about the situation. Be sure to give the reasons for your advice.

Letter 1

Dear Gazette Readers,
   I need your advice. I was in my neighborhood supermarket, going down the aisle of canned goods. There was an older woman in front of me, looking at the shelf. Suddenly, she put two cans of tuna fish into her bag and left the store. She didn't stop at the checkout counter! Seeing this woman steal food was very depressing for me. What should I do in a situation like this?

Ying

Letter 2

Dear Gazette Readers,
   I have a weekly test in my calculus course. Every week one student cheats on the test. I see him using his cell phone to photograph the paper of the student next to him. Then he uses the answers on his own test. I am very worried and confused. What should I do about this?

Luka

Step 1:   Getting Ideas

Read both letters. Discuss these questions with a partner.

Letter 1

1. What is the problem?

2. Why do you think the woman took the tuna fish?

3. Is it important to know her reason? Why or why not?

4. What happens to people who steal?

5. What should Ying do? Why?

Letter 2

1. What is the problem?

2. Is cheating on tests wrong? Why or why not?

3. Why should Luka care about the student who cheats?

4. Why do students cheat?

5. What should Luka do? Why?

Step 2:   Choosing the Letter

Choose the letter you want to answer.

Step 3:   Giving Advice and Stating Reasons

What do you think the writer of the letter should do? Give two or three reasons for your advice.

_____

_____

_____

You can use these words to organize the reasons in your letter.

first,	**first of all,**
second,	**in addition,**
finally,	**also,**

Write your advice in an informal letter.

Example:

Dear Anya,
   You are in a difficult situation. Your friends want you to stay up late every night to talk and listen to music. You want to study, but you do not know what to do. First of all, you should not join your friends every night. It's bad for your school work. Second, you should spend more time in the library, where you can study quietly. Finally, you should explain to your friends why you cannot always join them. True friends understand each others' wishes and needs.

A Friend

Step 4:   Revising

Work with a partner. Read each other's letters, and write comments in the margin. Use the checklist below. Don't worry about grammar errors.

> ## CHECKLIST FOR REVISING
>
> 1. Does the writing look like a letter?
> 2. Does the letter give advice?
> 3. Does the writer give reasons for the advice?
> 4. Does the writer organize the reasons clearly?

Review your writing. Do you want to change any part of your writing to make it clearer? Do you want to add any ideas?

Step 5: Editing—Fixing Comma Splices

A **comma splice** is an error. It happens when a writer puts a comma instead of a period between two separate sentences.

Comma Splices (Incorrect)
I think she is stealing, she should go to prison.
She is poor, she cannot pay for the house.

To correct a comma splice, change the comma to a period.

Correct
I think she is stealing. She should go to prison.
She is poor. She cannot pay for the house.

Work with a partner. Correct the comma splices in the letter of advice below.

Dear Mayor Clark,

I agree with you, Mr. Mayor. I am also very surprised at the way people behave in the ~~subway, young~~ subway. Young men rush to get the seats, they don't think about others. Elderly people are tired, they need a rest during the long train ride, pregnant women also need seats, my advice is to have an official card showing that a person is over 65, or disabled, or pregnant. That's a good way to stop all the arguments, people will have to get up from their seats, good manners will become the law.

Maggie Carlton

Read each sentence of your paragraph carefully. Edit any grammar errors you find. Use the checklist below.

CHECKLIST FOR EDITING
1. **Did you use the base form of the verb after *should*?**
2. **Did you use adjectives ending in *-ing* and *-ed* correctly?**
3. **Do you have any comma splices to fix?**

IV Additional Writing Opportunities

Choose one of the following topics and write a response of at least three sentences.

1. On a bus, someone is talking in a very loud voice into a cell phone. What should you do? Should you ask the person to stop? Why or why not?

2. "Money is the root of all evil."

   Do you agree or disagree that money causes very bad things to happen? Give two reasons. Give one example.

3. In a rich neighborhood, a woman sits at a table outside a supermarket. She says she is collecting money for an organization that helps poor children. In fact, this organization doesn't exist. The woman asks for money and keeps it all for herself.

   Should the police arrest this woman? Should she go to prison? Give two reasons for your opinion.

4. Would you like to work with "Habitat for Humanity"? Why or why not?

5. INTERNET RESEARCH: Search the Internet for the facts about homelessness in your area. What are the local government and other people doing about it? Give a short report to your class.

Journal Writing

In your journal, write a response to the following question. Don't worry about mistakes. Try to write half a page.

Do you need some advice for a situation in your life today? What is the situation? Why do you need advice?

3 CREATING GARDENS—BUILDING COMMUNITY

WRITING A FORMAL LETTER

In this unit you will practice:

- making requests and stating reasons
- using the future tense with *will*
- working with adverbs of manner
- using capital letters correctly

I Thinking About the Topic

> "I am very proud of our garden. It changed our neighborhood in many important ways. Gardens are great gifts that we should all have in our communities."
>
> Jose Coronado
> Bellerose Garden Project
> Bronx, New York

Look at the pictures and read the quote. Then think about these questions. Discuss your answers in small groups.

Compare the two pictures. What is the same? What is different? Why do you think people like to have gardens?

Reading for Writing

There are more than 750 community gardens in New York City. They are usually located in empty areas between apartment buildings. This is the story of one of these gardens.

PLANTING THE SEEDS OF GROWTH

We are a group of people of all ages who live in the Bronx, a part of New York City. We are working hard in our community garden to create an oasis[1] of greenery in our neighborhood.

We each have a small plot of land inside the garden. We plant our own
5 flowers, fruits, and vegetables. We water the plants regularly, and we patiently[2] watch them grow. Nature is often good to us, and the plants grow well. Then we happily reap[3] the benefits. In a good season, we harvest green peppers, zucchini, lettuce, tomatoes, cucumbers, blueberries, strawberries, and watermelons.

10 We have many visitors at the garden. Sometimes musicians come to play music. Experts on horticulture[4] also come to give us advice about gardening. During the school year, young students visit us and eagerly[5] study the plants and insects of the natural environment. Often on weekends, other people from the neighborhood come to sit quietly and
15 read. In the summer, we all watch movies together in the garden and talk about them afterwards.

Our garden is now another home for us. It brings us peace and quiet, and a sense of community. Years ago, before we all got together to create the garden, this area was full of garbage, rusty nails, rocks, and broken
20 glass. Now it's a beautiful place. We cannot imagine life without our garden now.

---

1. *oasis*: a place with water in the desert; a pleasant place in an area that is generally unpleasant
2. *patiently*: waiting calmly without getting upset
3. *reap*: get good things because of hard work; gather a crop such as wheat or corn
4. *horticulture*: the science of growing flowers, fruits, and vegetables
5. *eagerly*: with great interest and desire

General Understanding

1. Explaining Goals and Results

Complete these sentences with information from the reading. Compare answers with a partner.

1. The neighbors are working together because _____

   _____

2. In the past, the area was full of garbage, rusty nails, rocks, and broken

   glass. Now there are _____

   _____

2. Focusing on the Details

Work with a partner. Fill in the chart. For each category, list at least three activities that take place in the garden. Some activities may fit into more than one category.

Environmental (Gardening) Activities	Educational Activities	Social and Cultural Activities
1.	1.	1.
2.	2.	2.
3.	3.	3.

3. Your Turn

The city wants to turn an empty trash-filled area into a better place. They have two ideas:

1) build an office building

2) create a community garden

Write your response to the city's plans. Which plan do you like better? Explain why. Then take turns reading responses in small groups.

_____

_____

_____

_____

4. Open for Discussion

Think about these questions. Discuss your answers in small groups.

1. Would you like to work in a community garden? Why or why not?
2. What are the advantages of growing your own fruits and vegetables? What are the disadvantages?
3. Do you think it is important for cities to have gardens and parks? Why or why not?

After your discussions, choose one question and write your answer. Remember to write complete sentences.

_____

_____

_____

_____

_____

III Writing Focus

A. Language for Writing:
The Future Tense with *Will*

Use the future tense with *will* to make predictions, or guesses, about the future.

1. To form the future tense with *will*, use this pattern*:

$$will + base\ form$$
$$of\ the\ verb$$

My family and I	**will work**	in the community garden.
My father	**will plant**	fruits and vegetables.
My sisters	**will water**	them.
I	**will harvest**	them.

*Use the same pattern for all pronouns (*I, you, he/she/it, we, they*).

2. To form the negative, use this pattern:

$$will + not\ (\text{or other negative word})$$
$$+ base\ form\ of\ the\ verb$$

My family and I	**will not work**	in the hot sun.
	won't work	
My mother	**will never cut**	the flowers.

**We often use the contraction *won't* instead of the longer form, *will not*.

3. We often use certain words and expressions to refer to future time. Some of these are:

tomorrow
next week, month, year, etc.
in the future
soon
someday

1. Completing a Letter

Fill in the blanks in the letter. Use will *to form the future tense of the verbs in parentheses. Compare answers with a partner.*

Date ⟶ September 18, 2006

Salutation ⟶ Dear Mr. Diaz,

Body of the Letter ⟶ I know that you and your neighbors want to start a community garden, and I am writing to tell you about the benefits. In the future, with a garden in your area, you <u>will enjoy</u> *(enjoy)* many things. First, you and your
₁

neighbors _____ *(learn)* to work together. As a result,
₂

you _____ *(understand)* each other better. Second, you
₃

_____ *(save)* money on food. You _____
₄ ₅

(not/have to) buy all your fruits and vegetables. Also, with

more trees and plants, the air _____ *(be)* cleaner, and
₆

people _____ *(breathe)* more freely. In addition, the
₇

garden _____ *(become)* a wonderful "natural school."
₈

Children _____ *(come)* to the garden to learn about
₉

nature. Soon, people of all ages from all over town

_____ *(visit)* this beautiful natural space.
₁₀

Good luck with your garden!

Closing ⟶ Sincerely,

Signature ⟶ *Jose Coronado*

Printed Name ⟶ Jose Coronado

President, Bellerose Garden Project

2. Using the Future Tense with *Will*

Write at least three sentences about how your life will be in five years. Share your sentences with a partner.

_____

_____

_____

B. Words and Ideas: Adverbs of Manner

An adverb of manner describes the way someone does something or the way something happens. It answers the question *How?*

	VERB	ADVERB
The gardeners	**water**	**regularly**.
They all	**work**	**happily**.
The children	**study**	**eagerly**.
The plants	**grow**	**well**.

1. You can form most adverbs of manner by adding *-ly* to an adjective:

   beautiful ⟶ **beautifully**

2. For adjectives ending in *-y*, change *-y* to *-i* and add *-ly*:

   happy ⟶ **happily**

3. Some adverbs have irregular forms:

   good ⟶ **well**

4. For some adjectives and adverbs the form is the same, but the meaning is different:

   hard ⟶ **hard**

   The task is **hard**.   The gardeners are working **hard**.

   (The task is difficult.)   (The gardeners are doing a lot of work.)

   Note: **hardly** means "not very much."

   He hardly worked all day.

   (He didn't do much work.)

1. Completing Sentences

Work with a partner. Complete the sentences. Form adverbs of manner from the adjectives in parentheses.

1. Thanks to the garden, now we do not have much crime in our neighbor-

   hood. People walk _____ safely _____ (*safe*) on the streets.

2. In the morning, the garden is very peaceful. Sometimes I read

   _____ (*quiet*) under a tree.

3. Some of my neighbors work in the garden every day. They work

   _____ (*hard*) to take care of the plants.

4. Most of us don't have much money, but we _____

   (*happy*) give our time and energy to the garden.

5. We plant seeds in the spring, water them _____

   (*regular*) all summer, and harvest delicious vegetables in the fall.

6. Some plants take a long time to grow, but we wait

   _____ (*patient*) for the harvest.

7. We are very proud of our colorful flowers. The vegetables are also

   growing _____ (*beautiful*).

8. Although we are all very different, we all work _____

   (*good*) together.

2. Using Adverbs of Manner

Write three sentences about something you like to do in your free time. Use at least three adverbs of manner. Share your sentences with a partner.

_____

_____

_____

_____

Write a letter to a government official. Ask him or her to help you start a community garden in your neighborhood.

ALTERNATIVE TASK: In your letter, ask a government official to make some improvement in your neighborhood. For example, it could be a day-care center, a community pool, a tutoring program, or an after-school sports program.

Step 1:   Getting Ideas

1. Decide on your purpose: <u>What</u> do you want to write about?
<u>Who</u> will you write to?

Example: I want to write about a Halloween parade.
I want to write to Mayor John Rogers.

MY PURPOSE

I want to write about _____.

I will write to _____.

2. Make notes about the benefits of your project. Then group your ideas in categories.

Example: A Halloween Parade

Social and Cultural Benefits	Economic Benefits	Environmental Benefits
• fun for everyone • meet neighbors • enjoy an American holiday	good business for neighborhood stores—sell food and decorations	no cars—cleaner and safer

MY NOTES

_____

_____

_____

_____

Creating Gardens—Building Community

Step 2:   Supporting Your Ideas

Complete the first sentence below with the name of your project and one future benefit it will bring. Then add at least two more sentences with other benefits.

In the future, with a _____[project]_____ in our neighborhood,

_____

_____

_____

Step 3:   Writing the Letter

Now write your letter. Follow the directions below.

1. Use correct format. Look back at page 30 and review the key parts of the letter: date, salutation, body, closing, signature, and printed name.

2. At the beginning of the letter, explain your purpose.

Example: I am writing to ask for your help with a Halloween parade.

3. Explain the benefits of your project. Give at least two reasons or explanations.

4. End the letter with a new paragraph: Thank you for your help.

5. Sign the letter above your printed name, under the closing.

Step 4:   Revising

Work with a partner. Read each other's letters, and write comments in the margin. Use the checklist below. Don't worry about grammar errors.

> ### CHECKLIST FOR REVISING
>
> **1. Does the letter include all the key parts? Are there any parts missing?**
>
> **2. Does the first sentence explain the purpose of the letter?**
>
> **3. Does the letter clearly explain the benefits of the project?**

Review your writing. Do you want to change any part of the letter to make it clearer? Do you want to add any ideas?

Step 5: Editing—More Rules on Capitalization

Use capital letters for:

- **months and days of the week:**
  July, September, Sunday, Monday, Tuesday

- **names of streets and buildings:**
  Heath Avenue, City Hall

- **names of people, places, holidays:**
  Jose Coronado, Bronx, New York, Halloween

- **salutations, titles, and closings:**
  Dear Mr. Mayor, Mrs., Ms., Professor, Sincerely

There are 16 errors of capitalization in this letter. The first one is corrected for you. Find 15 more errors and correct them. Compare answers with a partner.

A
august 14, 2006

dear mayor black,

I am writing to ask for your help. We want to organize a halloween parade for the children in our neighborhood. The teachers and parents from bayside high school will help us. We want to march from maple street to sixth avenue on friday, october 31. Please help us get permission for this parade.

Thank you for your help.

sincerely,

Patricia Kopernic

Patricia Kopernic,

president, Bayside Beautification Group

Read each sentence of your letter carefully. Edit any grammar errors you find. Use the checklist below.

CHECKLIST FOR EDITING

1. **Did you use the future tense with *will* correctly?**
2. **Did you form adverbs of manner correctly?**
3. **Did you follow the rules of capitalization?**

Additional Writing Opportunities

Choose one of the following topics and write a response of at least three to four sentences.

1. Would you like to work on a community project? Perhaps you can tutor children in reading or math, work in a soup kitchen, become a Big Brother or Big Sister, or work on another project. Choose a project and explain your choice.

2. Write a letter to a friend. Describe your neighborhood. Describe the important places that bring people together: the library, the stores, the mall, schools, churches or other religious places. What improvements does your neighborhood need?

3. What lessons do you think working in a garden can teach people about living a good life? How can working in a garden teach people to be better people?

4. INTERNET RESEARCH: People use herbs for many purposes. They grow herbs for medicine, or to put in food. What kinds of herbs do people grow in other cultures? How do they grow these herbs? How do they use them? Search the Internet for the information, and write a brief report.

 Journal Writing

In your journal, write a response to the following question. Try to express yourself as well as you can. Don't worry about your mistakes. Try to write half a page.

What brings you peace and quiet in your mind or heart?

WRITING ABOUT THE PAST

In this unit you will practice:
- writing a narrative paragraph
- using the simple past tense
- working with prefixes
- using correct punctuation

I Thinking About the Topic

Look at the photograph by the famous American photographer Lewis Hine (1874–1939). Then do the following task in small groups.

Imagine that you can ask these children some questions. Write three questions.

_____

_____

_____

II ▸ Reading for Writing

During the early years of the United States, most children worked on farms. Later, industries began to grow, and poor children, as young as five years old, worked long hours every day in the factories. They were not able to go to school.

CHILDREN AT WORK

1835	Three thousand children went on strike[1] in the silk and cotton factories in Paterson, New Jersey. They wanted to get an 11-hour work day and a 6-day work week, but they were unsuccessful.
1903	"Mother" Jones[2] became famous in the fight for workers' rights. She led a march of child workers from clothing factories in Pennsylvania. They wanted a 55-hour work week.
1916–1919	Congress passed laws to ban[3] child labor. The courts said these laws were illegal because they interfered with[4] businesses.
1924	Congress suggested an amendment[5] to the U.S. Constitution that banned child labor. Only 26 of the 36 states approved the amendment, and it didn't become a law.
1938	The U.S. finally got a national law against child labor. This law is still in effect today. Businesses cannot employ children under 16 years old. Children from 16 to 18 can work only after school or on vacations. They cannot work at dangerous jobs.

---

1. *strike*: a period of time when workers stop working because they want better pay and working conditions
2. *"Mother" Jones (1837–1930)*: a labor leader who organized workers into unions, or groups, to fight for their rights
3. *ban*: say that something is not allowed
4. *interfere with* (someone or something): stop or limit
5. *amendment*: an addition to the U.S. Constitution

General Understanding

1. True or False?

Read these statements. Mark them T (true) or F (false). Compare answers with a partner.

_____ 1. It took the United States only a few years to ban child labor.

_____ 2. Children in the factories worked long hours after school.

_____ 3. Child workers worked more than 40 hours a week.

_____ 4. Today child labor is legal in some states in the U.S.

2. Explaining Reasons

Match the sentence beginnings with the sentence endings in the box. Compare answers with a partner.

1. Congress wanted to stop child labor __C__

2. Parents sent their children to work in the factories _____

3. Employers in business used child workers _____

4. The children went on strike _____

a. because they wanted better working conditions.

b. because children were cheap labor.

c. because children should go to school.

d. because they needed the money.

3. Your Turn

The United Nations document on "The Rights of Children" says that all nations should give each child:

- the right to health care
- the right to a decent standard of living (enough food, clothing, and housing)
- the right to protection from war
- the right to an education
- the right to play and rest

Discuss the list of rights with your class. What does each right mean? Then choose one right, and explain why you think it is important.

_____

_____

_____

4. Open for Discussion

Think about these questions. Discuss your answers in small groups.

1. What can you learn from having a job after school or on weekends?

2. What are the advantages of having a job and going to college at the same time? What are the disadvantages?

3. What kind of job would you like to have?

After your discussions, choose one question and write your answer. Remember to write complete sentences.

_____

_____

_____

III ◆ Writing Focus

A. Language for Writing: The Simple Past Tense

Use the simple past to write about conditions or actions that ended in the past.

Two million children **worked** in U.S. industries in 1911.

1. To form the simple past of most **regular verbs**, add *-d/-ed* to the base form of the verb.

   The children **lived** difficult lives.
   The children **worked** hard.

2. Some common examples of **irregular** simple past forms are:

   be
   Factory work **was** tiring.
   Sometimes the jobs **were** dangerous.

   have
   Children **had** many responsibilities.

   take
   Hines **took** pictures of children at work.

   go
   Sometimes workers **went** on strike.

3. To form **questions**, use *did* + base form of the verb for both regular and irregular verbs.

   Did they **work** long hours?
   Did they **have** happy lives?

4. To form **negative statements** with regular or irregular verbs, use *did* + *not* + base form of the verb.

   The workers **did not earn** a lot of money.
   The workers **didn't earn** a lot of money.

Using the Simple Past

Read these paragraphs about Lewis Hine's life. Fill in the blanks with the correct form of the simple past. Check your answers in a dictionary.

Seeing Is Believing

For most of my life, my job was doing my favorite thing in the world: taking photographs. I ____was____ *(be)* born in Oshkosh,

¹

Wisconsin, in 1874. At age 17, after high school, I _____ *(be)*

²

completely unskilled, and I _____ *(have/not)* any work

³

experience. My first jobs _____ *(be)* furniture mover,

⁴

salesman, and janitor. At the age of 25, I finally _____ *(go)* to

⁵

college and _____ *(become)* a teacher. At my first job, I

⁶

_____ *(begin)* an after-school camera club and _____

⁷ ⁸

(learn) photography with my students. I _____ *(decide)* to use

⁹

my photographs as a teaching tool. There _____ *(be)* millions

¹⁰

of immigrants coming to the U.S. in 1904. Through my pictures, I

_____ *(help)* my students understand the courage of the

¹¹

immigrants and the difficulties they faced.

In 1910, the National Child Labor Committee _____

¹²

(ask) me to help them. My wife and I _____ *(travel)* all over

¹³

the country to take pictures of child workers. The factory owners

_____ *(be)* angry. They _____ *(want/not)* photogra-

¹⁴ ¹⁵

phers to see the children, and sometimes it _____ *(be/not)*

¹⁶

safe to take pictures. But I _____ *(stop/not)* because I

¹⁷

_____ *(know)* that my pictures told a powerful story. I

¹⁸

wanted to make a change in this country with my photographs.

After all, seeing is believing!

B. Words and Ideas:
Negative Prefixes: *un-, dis-, in-, il-, im-*

A **prefix** is a group of letters that we can put in front of a word to change the meaning of the word.

Carl is employed.	=	He has a job.
Bill is **un**employed now.	=	He doesn't have a job now.

The prefixes *un-, dis-, in-, il-,* and *im-* mean "not." They usually turn a word into its antonym, or opposite.

un- + adjective
unhappy: sad
unhealthy: harmful, sickly

dis- + adjective
dishonest: not truthful

in-* + adjective
inhumane: treating people or animals in a cruel way

il- + many adjectives starting with *l***
illegal: against the law

im- + many adjectives starting with *p***
impossible: not possible; can't happen

**in-* does not always mean "not." It can also mean "into." For example, *income* means money that you receive regularly, or money that comes in.

**There are exceptions to the rule about *l-* and *p-*. For example, *unlimited* and *unprotected*.

Using Negative Prefixes

Write the antonyms of these words. Compare answers with a partner.

employed _____   humane _____

happy _____   legal _____

healthy _____   possible _____

honest _____   skilled _____

Fill in the blanks in the sentences with the antonyms from the list above. Compare answers with a partner.

1. Lewis Hine felt that child labor was cruel and ____inhumane____.

2. Without a good education, it is almost _____ to get a good job.

3. Because of _____ conditions in the cotton factories, child workers often got sick and died.

4. Some _____ employers lied about the age of the children in their factories.

5. In bad times, there was not enough work for adults. Many people were _____.

6. The work was hard, and the dark factories were depressing. The children were very _____.

7. _____ workers have no special knowledge or training.

8. Congress finally passed laws that made it _____ for children to miss school because of work.

YOUR TASK

Write a paragraph about a job you had in the past. For example, you can write about working in a supermarket, taking care of an older person, babysitting, or doing jobs around the house.

ALTERNATIVE TASK: Write a paragraph about your childhood. You can write about the places where you lived, your activities, your family, and your school.

Step 1:   Getting Ideas

A narrative paragraph tells a story. Narrative paragraphs usually tell *who, what, where, when, why,* and *how.*

Think about these questions and take notes on the answers.

TASK: My Job

1. How old were you when you had the job? _____

2. What were your duties or responsibilities? _____

_____

3. Did you like the work? Why or why not? _____

_____

4. What did you learn? _____

_____

ALTERNATIVE TASK: My Childhood

1. Where did you live? _____

2. How did you get along with your family and friends? _____

_____

3. What did you enjoy doing? _____

_____

4. What was your life like at school? _____

_____

Step 2: From Notes to Paragraph

Write sentences from your notes and form a paragraph.

Step 3: Choosing a Topic Sentence

Most paragraphs begin with a topic sentence. The **topic sentence** focuses on the main idea of a paragraph; it should not be too general. It should include the writer's thoughts or feelings about the topic.

TOPIC SENTENCES:

I am going to write about my favorite job.	too general
My favorite job was taking photographs.	good focus
My job was doing my favorite thing in the world: photography.	good focus and fun to read

Work with a partner. Put a check (✔) next to the sentences that are good topic sentences. Explain your answers.

_____ 1. My summer job was great.

_____ 2. My work taught me to be patient with young children.

_____ 3. My job in the family business was hard and boring.

_____ 4. I was never a lonely child because I had six dogs.

_____ 5. I am going to write about my family.

Now write an interesting topic sentence for your paragraph.

Step 4: Revising

Work with a partner. Read each other's paragraphs, and write comments in the margin. Use the checklist below. Don't worry about grammar errors.

CHECKLIST FOR REVISING

1. Put a check (✓) next to the topic sentence. Does this sentence focus on the main idea of the paragraph?

2. Does it tell you the author's thoughts or feelings about the topic?

Review your writing. Do you want to change any part of the paragraph to make it clearer? Do you want to add any ideas?

Step 5: Editing—Punctuation Rules

1. Use a **period** after a statement and after most abbreviations.

   I spent my childhood in Chile.
   Mr. Mrs. Ms. Dr. Ave. U.S.

2. Use a **question mark** after a question.

   How many hours did you work?

3. Use an **exclamation point** after a sentence that expresses excitement or surprise.

   I spent my first paycheck in one night!

4. Use a **comma** to separate items in a series.

   The factory was dark, hot, and uncomfortable.

Fill in the blanks in this paragraph with the correct punctuation. If no punctuation is necessary, write X. Compare answers with a partner.

My Job

This summer I had the coolest job. I worked for Juno Enterprises _X_₁ on 57th St __₂ and 6th Ave__₃ It's one of the largest entertainment companies in the U__₄S__₅ Lots of singers__₆ actors__₇ and musicians came into the office every day. Sometimes I even saw big TV stars __₈ I made photocopies__₉ and delivered packages__₁₀ Ms__₁₁ Young __₁₂ was my manager __₁₃ She made me wear a boring suit every day, but I didn't mind__₁₄ That's the way you dress for success__₁₅ Why did I work so hard__₁₆ I want to be a manager in a company like this someday __₁₇ Who knows__₁₈

Read each sentence of your paragraph carefully. Edit any grammar errors you find. Use the checklist below.

> ## CHECKLIST FOR EDITING
>
> 1. **Did you use the simple past for actions or conditions that ended in the past?**
>
> 2. **Did you use correct punctuation?**

 # IV Additional Writing Opportunities

Choose one of the following topics and write a response of one paragraph.

1. Write a paragraph about the childhood of a parent or relative. How was it different from your childhood? (Remember to use the simple past for actions or conditions that ended in the past.)

2. "We believe children have the right to play and dream, the right to normal sleep at night, the right to an education so that we may all have equality of opportunity."—National Child Labor Committee, 1913

   Write a paragraph about what rights you think children should have. Explain why they should have these rights.

3. "One picture is worth a thousand words."

   Explain what this saying means. Do you agree or disagree? Give some examples.

4. Do you like to take photographs? Describe your best photographs. What do you like to take pictures of? Where do you like to take pictures? Describe the photographs that are important to you.

5. INTERNET RESEARCH: Search the Internet for information about child labor laws in a country of your choice. Make a poster about this topic for the class.

 ## Journal Writing

Interview a parent or a person you know who has children. In your journal, write answers to the following questions. Don't worry about your mistakes. Try to write half a page.

What was this person's childhood like? Did any childhood experiences help this person become a good parent? What did he or she learn?

5 FREE AS A BIRD

WRITING DESCRIPTIONS

In this unit you will practice:
- writing a descriptive paragraph
- using verb tenses correctly
- working with prepositions and prepositional phrases
- using *its* and *it's* correctly

Thinking About the Topic

Look at the pictures. Then think about these questions. Discuss your answers in small groups.

Where do you think the animals seem happy? Why?
What do you think animals bring to our lives?

Reading for Writing

Emile Zola was a writer who lived in France at the end of the 19th century.

THE SPARROWS AT THE ZOO
by Emile Zola

Some people go to the zoo to look at the imprisoned animals. I go there to look at the birds, those free spirits that fly all around in broad daylight. There is nothing sadder than those wild animals with their large dreamy eyes, moving around in their cages in despair.[1] There is nothing happier
5 than those energetic and noisy sparrows, flying in and out of the prisons with songs of triumph.[2] The birds enter and leave the cages without fear. They celebrate the open skies and fresh air. As they fill up the cages with the sights and sounds of freedom, they bring great sadness to the poor prisoners.

10 One day, I saw a huge lion, his strong head stretched out on his paws. He[3] was looking at a sparrow that was flying about cheerfully through the bars of his cage. The wild beast's deep-set eyes were dreamy and moist. You could read in his eyes a sweet, sad daydream of the wide, open spaces of his homeland.

1. *despair:* a feeling of sadness with no hope
2. *triumph:* great success
3. Note: We usually refer to animals with the pronoun it, but we can use he and she for household pets. Zola uses he for the lion in this story because the writer is showing a close relationship between animal and human behavior.

General Understanding

1. Main Idea

Think about these questions. Then discuss your answers with a partner.

1. Choose the word(s) that describe a lion in its natural environment.

   a) strong   **b) unimportant**   **c) dominant**

2. Choose the word(s) that describe a bird in its natural environment.

   a) strong   **b) fragile**   **c) weak**

3. Zola sees things differently. Compare the lion and the birds in Zola's description.

The birds are _____.

The lion is _____.

2. Agree or Disagree?

Do you agree or disagree with these statements? Write A (agree) or D (disagree). Explain your answers to a partner. You may have different opinions.

_____ 1. Visiting a zoo makes Zola sad.

_____ 2. Without freedom, being strong means nothing.

_____ 3. The sparrows are happy because they are unimportant.

_____ 4. Prison teaches us to love freedom.

_____ 5. Daydreams are only for the weak and powerless.

3. Your Turn

Work in small groups. Discuss these ideas about the meaning of freedom. Do you agree or disagree?

- Freedom is the flight of a bird.

- Freedom is the right to make your own choices in life.

- Freedom is being able to say what you believe.

- Freedom is doing what you want to do.

What does freedom mean to you? Do you need money to be free? Do you need confidence in yourself? Write your ideas and explain them.

_____

_____

_____

_____

4. Open for Discussion

Think about these questions. Discuss your answers in small groups.

1. Why do we create public zoos?

2. How can we make zoos more comfortable for the animals?

3. Do you have a pet at home? Describe your pet's personality. OR Imagine that you have a pet and describe it.

4. How can pets help people of all ages? Give examples.

5. Some people have wild animals like lions and tigers and poisonous snakes as pets. Should we allow this? Is it fair to the animals? Is it fair to the community?

After your discussions, choose one question and write a response. Remember to write complete sentences.

_____

_____

_____

Writing Focus

A. Language for Writing: Using Correct Verb Tenses

1. Use the **simple present tense** to write about a regular act or habit, thoughts, feelings, and general facts.

   Michael Mountain **works** with animals.

   Some time expressions that go with the simple present are:

   today, this year, at present, now

2. Use the **simple past** to write about conditions or actions that ended in the past.

   He **started** a shelter for animals in 1986.

   Some time expressions that go with the simple past are:

   last year, in the past, _____ years/months/weeks ago

3. Use the **future with** *will* to make predictions about the future.

   He **will enlarge** the shelter next year.

   Some time expressions that go with *will* for the future are:

   in the future, until _____ (a future date)

1. Choosing the Correct Verb Tense

Circle the correct tense of the verb in each sentence. Compare answers with a partner.

1. Michael Mountain *(is, was)* born in England.

2. Many years ago, the five-year-old Michael Mountain *(goes, went)* fishing with his grandfather.

3. Michael *(sees, saw)* a little fish on his hook. He threw the fish back in the water.

4. He said to his grandfather, "In the future, I *(help, will help)* animals who are hurt and in pain."

5. Michael *(marries, married)* an American woman and bought a ranch in Utah in 1983.

6. Now Michael Mountain often *(speaks, spoke)* in public about the importance of kindness to animals.

2. Completing Paragraphs

Fill in the blanks in the paragraphs below with the correct form of the verb. You can use the simple present, simple past, or future tense with will.

In 1983, a group of friends __started__ *(start)* "Best Friends" Animal Sanctuary" in Utah's Red Rock country. Today, the sanctuary, *(be)* _____ a no-kill animal haven[1] of 350 acres with 1500 dogs, cats, rabbits, horses, goats, and other animals. It _____ *(accept)* hurt and homeless animals. Michael Mountain, the president of the organization, says that their sanctuary _____ *(continue)* taking care of animals until they die. The sanctuary's idea is simple. Mountain says, "Kindness to animals _____ *(make)* the world a better place for all of us."

At present, volunteers[2] _____ *(come)* to "Best Friends" from all over the United States. They _____ *(spend)* their vacations washing out food bowls, walking dogs, cleaning litter boxes, and sometimes just holding hurt and frightened animals. Last year, 5000 volunteers _____ *(visit)* "Best Friends" to help out with the animals.

---

1. *haven:* a safe place; a shelter
2. *volunteer:* someone who works without pay

B. Words and Ideas:
Prepositions and Prepositional Phrases

Prepositions are words that show place, time, topic, description, and possession. They include *at, in, on, about, with, without,* and *of*.

Prepositional phrases consist of a preposition and a following noun or noun phrase. Some examples are:

Place	Time	Topic
at home	**in** 2006	(teach) **about** animal life
in Canada	**on** July 4th	(talk) **about** zoos
	at 3 o'clock	

Description	Possession
(a lion) **with** dreamy eyes	(the name) **of** the zoo
(a cage) **with** no light	
(a cat) **without** a tail	

1. Completing Sentences

Work with a partner. Fill in the blanks in the sentences with the correct prepositions.

1. People are talking ___about___ the future of zoos. The question is:

   Should we put animals _____ zoos?

2. Some people say "no." They do not like to see wild animals

   _____ cages _____ big bars.

3. Other people like zoos. They take their children to the zoo to teach them

   _____ wildlife. They can also learn the names _____

   many unusual animals.

4. There are some new zoos _____ bars or cages. The animals can

   move around freely and feel _____ home.

5. The Vincennes Zoo _____ Paris, France, opened _____

   1934. It had no cages.

6. _____ April 22, 1998, the Disney Company opened a new animal

   park _____ Florida. Its name is Wild Kingdom.

7. There are some modern zoos _____ special features that make the

   visit fun. For example, a zoo _____ Canada has periscopes[1] so

   that people can see the world like a giraffe.

8. Some animal parks are expensive. Only people _____ a lot of

   money can make the trip. But there are also many interesting zoos

   _____ big admissions fees.

2. Using Prepositions and Prepositional Phrases

Read the question below and write your answer. Use three prepositions or prepositional phrases in your answer. Then share your answers in small groups.

We have zoos for three reasons: Zoos help us protect animals; they teach people about wildlife; and they provide entertainment. Which reason is most important to you? Why?

_____

_____

_____

_____

---

1. periscope: a long tube with mirrors that you use to look over the top
   of something

Write a descriptive paragraph about your pet. What does your pet look like? Describe its activities. How do you feel about your pet? OR Imagine that you have a pet. Describe it, and tell why this is the perfect pet for you.

ALTERNATIVE TASK: Write a descriptive paragraph about a zoo you know. Does it have cages or does it have open areas for the animals? Include your ideas and feelings about the zoo. OR Write about your idea of the perfect zoo.

Step 1:   Getting Ideas

Look at the cluster diagrams below. They show one way you can brainstorm, or get ideas.

TASK:

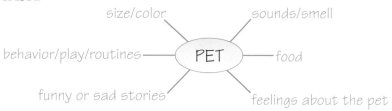

ALTERNATIVE TASK:

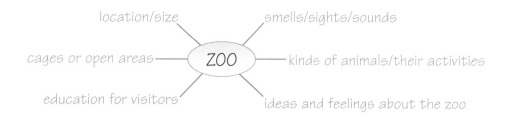

Make a cluster diagram for your ideas. Then choose the best ideas for your paragraph.

Step 2:   From Notes to Paragraph

A descriptive paragraph should be specific. That means it should contain details. Many of the details often relate to our senses: sight, sound, smell, touch, and taste. For example:

The night our cat died I heard only my	sound
mom's quiet crying. She sat by him, watching	sight
his sad eyes, gently petting his soft fur.	touch

Step 3:   Choosing a Title and a Topic Sentence

The **title** usually tells the subject of the paragraph. A good title makes the reader want to keep reading.

Put a check (✓) next to the interesting titles. Discuss your answers with a partner.

_____ a.   Cruel Cages   _____ c.   My Dog Skip

_____ b.   A Zoo   _____ d.   Total Love

The **topic sentence** tells the main idea of the paragraph.

Put a check (✓) next to the interesting topic sentences. Discuss your answers with a partner.

_____ 1. Even a bad zoo can change.

_____ 2. As a child, I never liked going to the zoo.

_____ 3. My dog taught me responsibility and love.

_____ 4. Pets can be nice.

_____ 5. My grandmother's tiny dog helps her more than all the medicine in the world.

Now write an interesting title and topic sentence and complete your paragraph.

Step 4:   Revising

Work with a partner. Read each other's paragraphs, and write comments in the margin. Use the checklist below. Don't worry about grammar errors.

CHECKLIST FOR REVISING

1. **Does the paragraph have an interesting title?**

2. **Does the topic sentence focus on the main idea of the paragraph?**

3. **Are there enough specific details that make the readers "see" and "feel" the description?**

Review your writing. Do you want to change any part of the paragraph to make it clearer? Do you want to add any ideas?

Step 5:   Editing—*Its* and *It's*

1. *Its* is a possessive form.

   The lion rested **its head** on **its paws**.
   (The head and the paws belong to the lion.)

   This sentence is difficult. **Its meaning** isn't clear.
   (The meaning of the sentence isn't clear.)

2. *It's* is a contraction for *It is*.

   It's sad to see the big lion in a tiny cage.
   (It is sad to see this situation.)

   The lion is roaring. **It's** making noise because it's hungry.
   (It is making noise.)

Correct the errors in the sentences below.

1. I saw a beautiful cat. ~~It's~~ Its paws were all white.

2. Its not fair to kill animals that don't have homes.

3. An animal gives you all it's love.

4. Have you read "The Bird Man of Alcatraz"? Its the story of a man who learns about love by taking care of birds.

5. It feels good to hold a puppy. It's fur is very soft.

6. Its important to understand our relationship with nature.

Read each sentence of your paragraph carefully. Edit any grammar errors you find. Use the checklist below.

CHECKLIST FOR EDITING

1. **Did you use the simple past, the simple present, and the future with *will* correctly?**

2. **Did you use the correct prepositions and prepositional phrases?**

3. **Did you use *its* and *it's* correctly?**

IV Additional Writing Opportunities

Choose one of the following topics and write a response of one paragraph.

1. Many animal shelters keep animals only for a short time. They kill animals that nobody wants. "Best Friends" keeps the animals and never kills them. How do you feel about the "Best Friends" way of doing things?

2. Do all societies have household pets? Are there countries where people don't usually have pets? Where? Choose a country you know. What pets are popular in that culture?

3. "People have the right to enjoy four freedoms: freedom from want (freedom from being poor), freedom from fear, freedom of speech, freedom of religion."—Franklin Delano Roosevelt

   Which of these four freedoms do you think is the most important? Explain your answer.

4. "Stone walls do not a prison make, nor iron bars a cage."—William Shakespeare

   Not all prisons have bars or walls. Some prisons are psychological—they are only in the mind. For example, a bad memory or a fear of something can be a prison in the mind. Describe a prison in the mind that stops you or someone you know from being free.

5. INTERNET RESEARCH: Many animals are in danger of becoming extinct, or dying out. Some of these endangered animals are the tiger, the panda, the koala in Australia, the whale, the turtle, or the rhinoceros. Search the Internet for one of these animals. Make a poster that answers these questions: 1) Why is the animal becoming extinct? 2) What are people doing about this problem?

 Journal Writing

In your journal, write a response to the following questions. Don't worry about your mistakes. Try to write half a page.

What was a time in your life when you felt free? Why was this time special for you?

6 EDUCATION: GRAPHING PROGRESS

WRITING ABOUT GRAPHS

In this unit you will practice:

- writing a paragraph to explain a graph
- comparing data with *more ... than, fewer ... than, less ... than*
- working with words that explain data
- editing for subject/verb agreement

I ◆ Thinking About the Topic

Look at the pictures and think about the questions. Discuss your answers in small groups.

Do you enjoy reading? What are some of your favorite books? Do you like mysteries, romance books, history books, comic books, or books about people's lives? Do you think it is important to have libraries that are open to everyone? Explain.

II ▸ Reading for Writing

Statistics are groups of numbers that show facts or measurements. This graph gives statistics, or data, about literacy rates[1] in the world from 1960 to 2000. Literate people know how to read, write, and work with numbers. Study the graph and answer the questions that follow.

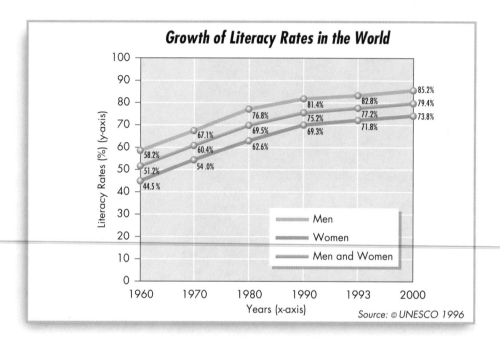

WHAT IS A GRAPH?

A graph is a "picture" of data with an x-axis and a y-axis. The x-axis is the horizontal line that goes from left to right on the bottom. The y-axis is the vertical line that goes from the top to the bottom on the side. A graph also has a legend that explains what the lines in the picture represent.

Work with a partner. Answer these questions.

1. What information does the x-axis show?

2. What information does the y-axis show?

3. How many groups, or categories, are in the legend? How many lines are on the graph?

4. According to the legend, what does each line show?

---

1. *rate*: how fast something changes; it can get bigger (go up), get smaller (go down), or stay the same during a certain period of time

General Understanding

1. Reading the Statistics: True or False?

Work with a partner. Mark these statements T (true) or F (false).

_____ 1. In 1960, about 50 percent (50%) of the people in the world knew how to read and write.

_____ 2. In 2000, 90 percent (90%) of the world's population were literate.

_____ 3. In 1960, at least 40 percent (40%) of men knew how to read and write and almost 60 percent (60%) of women were literate.

_____ 4. Literacy went up in the 1990s; it went down in the 1960s.

_____ 5. The difference between men's and women's literacy is becoming smaller as time goes on.

2. Thinking about Reasons

Which statements may be reasons for the data in the graph? Put a check (✓) next to them. Discuss your answers with a partner.

_____ 1. After 1960, there were important changes in women's lives.

_____ 2. Literacy rates went down because of local wars.

_____ 3. Building more schools helped the growth of literacy.

_____ 4. As businesses began to grow, there was a great need for literate workers.

_____ 5. Countries spent less money on education.

3. Your Turn

Think about your early school years. Did you like school then? Why or why not? What subjects did you like? What subjects did you hate? Who were your favorite teachers?

Write a few sentences about your school experiences. Then share your writing in small groups.

_____

_____

_____

4. Open for Discussion

Think about these questions. Discuss your answers in small groups.

1. Some families don't send their children to school. They prefer to teach the children at home. Would you like to be "home-schooled"? Why or why not?

2. Women with more education usually don't have a lot of children. Can you think of some reasons to explain this fact?

3. People who can read and write are better citizens. Do you agree or disagree?

4. People in all countries will have a good life when everyone in the world knows how to read and write. Do you agree or disagree?

After your discussions, choose one statement and write your ideas. Remember to write complete sentences.

_____

_____

_____

_____

III ▸ Writing Focus

A. Language for Writing: Comparing Statistics

1. Use *more…than* to show that the data on one item are higher or greater than the data on another item.

   More people in 2000 **than** in 1960 knew how to read and write.

2. Use *fewer…than* or *less…than* to show that the data on one item are lower than the data on another item.

   There were **fewer** educational **opportunities*** for people in 1960 **than** in 2000. There was **less literacy**** in the world in 1960 **than** in 2000.

   *Use *fewer…than* for **count nouns**, nouns that have both singular and plural forms. Use the plural forms to compare them: teachers, opportunities, countries, people, men, women, etc.

   Use *less…than* for **non-count nouns, nouns that usually have only singular forms: literacy, education, knowledge, progress, growth, money, etc.

Using *More … than, Fewer … than, Less … than*

Work with a partner. Fill in the blanks with more…than, fewer…than, *or* less…than. *Use the information you learned in this unit. Look back at the world literacy graph on page 62 to check your answers.*

1. Many _____more_____ people in the world knew how to read and write in 2000 ____than____ in 1960.

2. We can see good progress in world literacy from 1960 to 2000. In the earlier years there were _____ literate men and women _____ in later years.

3. There was _____ growth in women's literacy _____ in men's literacy from 1960 to 2000.

4. Why was there _____ world literacy in 2000 _____ in 1960? The graph does not explain this.

5. The reason may be because people around the world had _____ educational opportunities after 1960 _____ before 1960.

6. The growth of world literacy is good news. People with _____ knowledge can help the world better _____ people with _____ knowledge.

B. Words and Ideas: Analyzing Statistics

1. Matching Words and Meanings

Match the words in the left column with their meanings in the right column.

___b___ 1. decrease   a. the way a situation is changing

_____ 2. increase   b. going down in numbers

_____ 3. percent   c. going up in numbers

_____ 4. total   d. a part of 100

_____ 5. trend   e. whole amount, the sum of all the parts

2. Completing a Paragraph

Work with a partner. Fill in the blanks in this paragraph with the words from the list in exercise B1.

Title →

Topic Sentence →

Source of Information →

Details and Comparisons →

Importance of the Graph to the Writer →

The Growth of Literacy Rates in the World

The graph "Growth of Literacy Rates in the World" gives important information about world literacy since 1960. UNESCO[1] collected the data for this graph. The graph shows a clear ___trend___ : World literacy is growing. For
                                         1
example, in 1960, 51.2 _____ of people were
                              2
literate. In 2000, 79.4 percent of the _____ adult
                                              3
population knew how to read and write.

This is an _____ of 28.2 percent. Also, in 1960,
                 4
there was a big difference between the percentage[2] of literate men and the percentage of literate women. However, the statistics for recent years show a

_____ in this difference. These changes are good
       5
because today we need more and more educated people to solve the world's problems.

---

1. The United Nations Educational, Scientific, and Cultural Organization
2. Note: Use *percentage* with *of* and a plural noun: *the percentage of literate men*. Use *percent* after a number: *51.2 percent*.

3. Discussing Statistics

Work with a partner. Study the bar graph. Then answer the questions below in complete sentences.

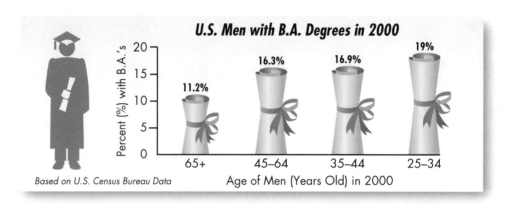

U.S. Men with B.A. Degrees in 2000

Based on U.S. Census Bureau Data

1. What is the topic of the graph?

_____

_____

2. What does the x-axis show? What does the y-axis show?

_____

_____

3. What is the general trend?

_____

_____

4. What do you think explains this trend?

_____

_____

5. How do you think the percentages of U.S. women with B.A. degrees compare with the percentages of U.S. men with B.A. degrees?

_____

_____

Write a paragraph about the information in the graph below on literacy in Latin America and the Caribbean.

ALTERNATIVE TASK: Write a paragraph on the information in the graph, "U.S. Women with B.A. Degrees in 2000," on the next page.

Step 1:   Getting Ideas

Decide which graph you want to write about. Then answer the questions below the graph you chose.

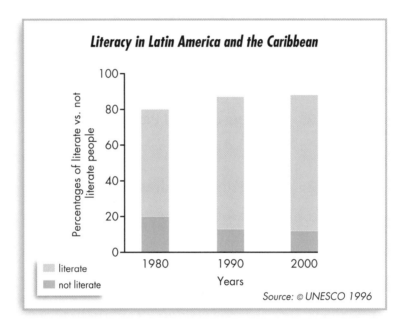

Literacy in Latin America and the Caribbean

Percentages of literate vs. not literate people

literate
not literate

Years

Source: © UNESCO 1996

1. What information does the graph show?

2. What is the source of the information? (Where does the information come from?)

3. What percentage of the population was literate in 1980, 1990, and 2000?

4. What percentage of the population was not able to read and write in 1980, 1990, and 2000?

5. Compare the graph with the graph on page 62. Are the trends similar or different?

6. Why is the information in the graph important?

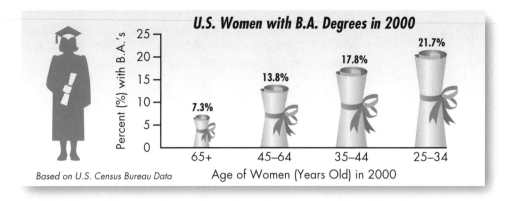

U.S. Women with B.A. Degrees in 2000

Based on U.S. Census Bureau Data

1. What information does the graph show?

2. What is the source of the information?

3. What is the general trend? Is the trend similar to or different from the trend in the graph on page 68?

4. Why is the information in the graph important?

Step 2:   Studying a Model Paragraph

Study the key parts of the paragraph on page 67.

Step 3:   Organizing the Paragraph

Now organize your sentences and write a paragraph. Use the model paragraph on page 67 as a guide.

Step 4:   Revising

Work with a partner. Read each other's paragraphs, and write comments in the margin. Use the checklist below. Don't worry about grammar errors.

> **CHECKLIST FOR REVISING**
>
> 1. **Does the topic sentence tell what the graph shows?**
>
> 2. **Does the writer give the source of the information?**
>
> 3. **Does the writer discuss the general trend? Are the details and comparisons good examples of this trend?**
>
> 4. **Does the writer tell why the information in the graph is important?**

Review your writing. Do you want to change any part of the paragraph to make it clearer? Do you want to add any ideas?

Step 5: Editing—Subject–Verb Agreement

The subject and the verb in a sentence have to agree with each other. Some examples in the simple present tense are:

Incorrect	Correct
I reads the newspaper often.	I **read** the newspaper often.
He have many books.	He **has** many books.
He learn new ideas quickly.	He **learns** new ideas quickly.
World literacy increase every year.	World literacy **increases** every year.

Look at the underlined subjects and verbs in the sentences below. Put a check (✓) next to the sentences with correct agreement. Correct the ones with errors.

1. The <u>graph show</u> information about education in the United States.

   graph shows

2. More <u>people gets</u> college degrees today than in the past. _____

3. <u>Education give</u> people many opportunities. _____

4. Without education, <u>people are</u> not able to improve their lives.

   _____

5. Today <u>men and women</u> in the U.S. <u>leads</u> better lives because of

   education. _____

6. The <u>lives</u> of people all over the world <u>needs</u> to be better. _____

Read each sentence of your paragraph carefully. Edit any grammar errors you find. Use the checklist below.

> **CHECKLIST FOR EDITING**
> 1. Did you use *more…than, fewer…than, less…than* correctly?
> 2. Did you use the words you learned to analyze the data?
> 3. Did you check for subject–verb agreement?

Additional Writing Opportunities

Choose one of the following topics and write a response of one paragraph.

1. Very few people finish college in the U.S. Why do you think this is true? Why do you want a college education?

2. Do you remember a favorite teacher? Why was this teacher special? Did this person teach well? How did he or she make you feel? Explain why you remember this teacher so well.

3. Why do you think it is much harder for an adult to learn to read and write than for a child?

4. In his autobiography, Malcolm X writes about how reading made him feel free when he was in prison. Do you see a connection between reading and freedom? Explain.

5. INTERNET RESEARCH: Search the Internet for a graph about education in your area or a country of your choice. Find information about one of the following topics: 1) high school graduates; 2) high school dropouts; 3) the numbers of students in primary schools, secondary schools, and colleges or universities. Explain the information on the graph.

 ## Journal Writing

In your journal, write a response to the following questions. Don't worry about mistakes. Try to write half a page.

What is an interesting book, play, magazine, newspaper, or comic strip that you are now reading? How is this reading material opening up a whole new world for you?

WRITING ABOUT A SHORT STORY

In this unit you will practice:

- writing an analysis of a short story
- using *want, would like,* and *ask*
- identifying noun and adjective word forms
- learning about word division

I Thinking About the Topic

Look at the pictures. Then think about this question. Discuss your answers in small groups.

What do you need to be happy? Name four things.

II ▸ Reading for Writing

The following story is a fable by Russian writer Leo Tolstoy (1828–1910). Tolstoy was famous for his novels *Anna Karenina* and *War and Peace*, but he also wrote short stories and fables. A fable is a short story that has a clear moral, or message, at the end.

THE KING AND THE SHIRT

A king once became ill.[1]

"I will give half my kingdom to the man who can cure[2] me," he said.

All the wise men[3] thought about how to cure the king. One of the wise men finally had an idea.

5 "Find a happy man, take his shirt, and put it on the king. Then the king will get better."

The king sent his bodyguards[4] to look for a happy man. They traveled all over the kingdom, but they could not find a happy man. There was no one who was completely satisfied. One man was wealthy, or rich, but he

10 was sick. Another man was healthy, but he was poor. Another was rich and healthy, but he had a bad wife. Other men had children, but the children were bad. Everyone had something to complain about.[5]

Finally late one night, the king's son was passing by a very poor area and he heard someone say:

15 "God be praised, I finished my work, I ate my fill,[6] and now I can lie down and sleep! What more could I want?"

The king's son told the bodyguards to take the poor man's shirt and bring it to the king. In exchange, the king's son wanted to give the man a lot of money.

20 The bodyguards went into the man's hut[7] to take off the man's shirt, but the happy man was so poor that he had no shirt.

---

1. *ill*: sick
2. *cure*: make healthy again
3. *wise men*: intelligent men; the king's advisers
4. *bodyguard*: a person whose job is to protect somebody
5. *complain about*: say that you are unhappy about something
6. *eat one's fill*: satisfy one's desire for food
7. *hut*: a small house with only one or two rooms

General Understanding

1. Summarizing the Story

Match the sentence beginnings with the sentence endings in the box to make true statements about the reading. Compare answers with a partner.

1. The king is unhappy _____

2. The king will give _____

3. The wise man says that _____

4. The king's son finds _____

5. The happy man cannot help _____

a. because he doesn't have a shirt.

b. because he is sick.

c. a happy man who is poor.

d. the shirt of a happy man will make the king better.

e. half his land to the person who cures him.

2. Thinking About the Moral of the Story

Work with a partner. Put a check (✓) next to the sentences that tell the moral, or message, of the story.

_____ 1. You cannot buy happiness.

_____ 2. Only poor people can be happy.

_____ 3. Kings should be wise.

_____ 4. You cannot take another person's happiness.

_____ 5. You can only find happiness for yourself.

3. Your Turn

The poor man is happy for three reasons:

- He completed his work for the day.
- He is not hungry.
- He has a bed to sleep in.

Could you be happy with the things that make the poor man happy? Compare your idea of happiness with his.

Write your answer. Work in small groups, Read your answers and compare ideas.

_____

_____

_____

_____

4. Open for Discussion

Think about these statements. Do you agree or disagree? Why? Discuss your answers in small groups.

1. People are never satisfied with what they have.
2. Happy people have nothing to complain about.
3. Without good health, happiness is not possible.
4. A rich person always has a happier life than a poor person.

After your discussions, choose one statement and write your ideas. Remember to write complete sentences.

_____

_____

_____

_____

III Writing Focus

A. Language for Writing:
Want, Would like, and *Ask*

1. You can use *want* or *would like* to express your wish or desire for something.

SUBJECT	VERB	INFINITIVE	
		to + base form	
I	want	to be	happy.
I	would like*	to help	the king.

2. To express your wish or desire for someone else, use this pattern:

SUBJECT	VERB	OBJECT**	INFINITIVE	
I	want	the king	to be	happy.
I	would like	him	to feel	better.

Ask also uses this pattern:

SUBJECT	VERB	OBJECT	INFINITIVE	
The king	asks	his bodyguards	to find	a happy man.

*In the simple past tense, use *want*; there is no simple past form for *would like*: I **wanted** to help the king.

**Remember, the object pronouns are: *me, you, him, her, it, us, them.*

1. Correcting Sentences

Study the verb forms in these sentences and correct the errors. Compare answers with a partner.

1. The king ~~wants be~~ healthy. _{wants to be}

2. The wise men wants help the king.

3. The king's son wants that his father feel better.

4. The poor man would like to helping the king.

5. The king's bodyguards ask the happy man give them his shirt.

2. Writing Sentences

Use the cues to write sentences about the characters in the fable. Be sure to use correct capitalization and punctuation.

1. king/want/feel better

The king wants to feel better.
_____

2. wise men/would like/king/be happy

_____

3. wise men/would like/find/a happy man

_____

4. rich man/would like/be healthy

_____

5. healthy man/want/have/more money

_____

6. king's son/ask/poor man/give/him/his shirt

_____

7. king's son/would like/give/poor man/a lot of money

_____

8. poor man/would like/help/king

_____

3. Using *Want* and *Would like*

Write five sentences about your wishes and desires in the next few years. Use want, would like, and the structures you learned in this unit. Share your sentences with a partner.

_____

_____

_____

_____

B. Words and Ideas: Adjective and Noun Forms

A **noun** is a person, place, thing or idea. An **adjective** describes a noun.

	ADJECTIVE	NOUN	
He is a	**sick**	**man.**	(person)
It is a	**wealthy**	**city.**	(place)
This is a	**beautiful**	**flower.**	(thing)
This is an	**important**	**thought.**	(idea)

An **adjective** tells how something or someone is.

	ADJECTIVE
The man is	**sick.**
The city is	**wealthy.**
The flower is	**beautiful.**
The thought is	**important.**

A **noun** tells what something or someone has.

	NOUN
The man has a	**sickness.**
The city has	**wealth.**
The flower has	**beauty.**
The thought has	**importance.**

Common Adjective and Noun Endings

Word endings are also called **suffixes**. Suffixes can help you identify adjectives and nouns and the relationships between them.

To turn some nouns into adjectives:

	NOUN		ADJECTIVE
1. Add -*y*	health	⟶	**healthy**
2. Add -*ful*	beauty	⟶	**beautiful***

To turn some adjectives into nouns:

	ADJECTIVE		NOUN
1. Add -*ness*	ill	⟶	**illness**
	happy	⟶	**happiness***
2. Replace -*ent*/-*ant*	intelligent	⟶	**intelligence**
with -*ence*/-*ance*	important	⟶	**importance**

*When the noun or adjective ends in -*y*, drop -*y* and add -*i*.

Choosing Adjective and Noun Forms

Work with a partner. Complete this paragraph. Circle the correct form of the word in parentheses.

Title →

An Analysis of Tolstoy's "The King and the Shirt"

Topic Sentence →

In his fable "The King and the Shirt," Leo Tolstoy writes about (*happy,* (*happiness*)). The story is about a (*sick, sickness*) king who the doctors cannot cure. The king's wise men ask him to find the shirt

Summary →

of a (*happy, happiness*) man for the king to wear. They think this will make the king's (*ill, illness*) go away. The bodyguards find a

Moral Opinion →

happy man, but he does not have a shirt. For me, the moral of this story is that you cannot take another person's happiness for yourself. I agree with this message. I say this because I have a very (*wealthy, wealth*) friend who is very (*ill, illness*). He has money to pay his doctors, but he spends his life in bed. Compared to my friend, Tolstoy's poor man is (*rich, richness*) because he has his (*healthy, health*). Fortunately, my friend understands the (*important, importance*) of enjoying the (*happy, happiness*) moments in his life. So, as Tolstoy suggests, we shouldn't try to "wear" another person's happiness. We each have to find our own.

YOUR TASK

Write an analysis of "Equal Inheritance," another fable by Tolstoy.

ALTERNATIVE TASK: **Choose another fable by Tolstoy, or one by a writer from another culture, and write an analysis of it.**

Step 1: Understanding the Parts of an Analysis

Study the analysis on page 80. Your paragraph should have:

1. a **title**.

2. a **topic sentence** with the author's name, the title of the story, and a statement of the theme. (The theme in "The King and the Shirt" is happiness.)

3. a **summary** that tells what the story is about in a few sentences.

4. a **moral**, or the message of the story.

5. your **opinion**: Do you agree with the story's message? Why or why not?

Step 2: Reading and Taking Notes for a Summary

Read this fable by Leo Tolstoy.

Equal Inheritance

A rich man had two sons. The older son was his favorite, and the man decided to leave all his money to him when he died. The mother felt sorry for her younger son. She asked her husband not to tell the boys about his plans.

One day the mother was sitting at the window and crying. A traveler came to the window and asked her why.

"How can I stop crying?" she said. "There is no difference between my two sons, but their father wants to leave everything to one of them and nothing to the other. I asked their father not to tell the boys this. But I have no money of my own to give my younger son."

Then the traveler said, "Tell your sons that the older brother will get all the money and the younger one will get nothing. Then they will be equal."

When the younger son learned that he wasn't going to get any money, he went to another country and he learned a trade.[1] The older son lived at home and learned nothing; he was sure about his future as a rich man.

When the father died, the older son did not know how to do anything. He spent all his money, and he became poor. But the younger son was prepared. He knew how to make money, and he became rich.

---

1. *trade*: a job you need special knowledge or skills for

To prepare your summary, answer these questions.

1. Why is the mother unhappy?

2. What is the traveler's advice?

3. What happens to the older son when his father dies?

4. What happens to the younger son?

Step 3:   Explaining the Moral of the Story

Put a check (✓) next to the statement that best tells the moral, or message, of the story. Then think of some other ways to express this moral. Share your ideas with a partner.

_____ 1. People who get everything from their parents never learn how to take care of themselves.

_____ 2. It is better to be born rich than poor.

Now write your analysis. Be sure to include all the key parts.

Step 4:   Revising

Work with a partner. Read each other's paragraphs. Use the checklist below, and write comments in the margin. Don't worry about grammar errors.

> ### CHECKLIST FOR REVISING
>
> 1. Does the analysis have a title?
>
> 2. Does the topic sentence include the author, title, and theme of the story?
>
> 3. Is the summary clear?
>
> 4. Does the writer explain the moral of the story well?
>
> 5. Does the writer give his or her opinion?

Review your writing. Do you want to change any part of the analysis to make it clearer? Do you want to add any ideas?

Step 5: Editing—Word Division

Sometimes a word at the end of a line is too long to fit. You can either write the whole word on the next line or divide the word by putting a hyphen (-) between the syllables. This process is also called hyphenation.

For example, sickness has two syllables: **sick·ness**

The king was ill, and nobody knew how to cure his sickness.

Some Rules of Word Division

1. Divide a word between its syllables. When you are not sure where the syllables are, check in a dictionary.

2. Don't divide a word that has only one syllable *(rich, sick)*.

3. Divide a word
   - after a vowel: **ho·nest**
   - between double consonants: **hap·py**

   But keep word roots together: **ill·ness**

4. Leave at least two letters on a line.
   Correct: **equa-lity**   Incorrect: **e-quality**

Put a check (✔) next to the correct word divisions. Then correct the word divisions that are incorrect.

_✔_ 1. great-ness	_____ 4. i-mportant	_____ 7. he-alth
_____ 2. ~~shi rt~~ shirt	_____ 5. happ-in-ess	_____ 8. joy-ful
_____ 3. kingd-om	_____ 6. e-verything	_____ 9. em-pty

Read each sentence of your paragraph carefully. Edit any grammar errors you find. Use the checklist below.

CHECKLIST FOR EDITING

1. Did you use *want, would like,* and *ask* correctly?

2. Did you use adjective and noun word forms correctly?

3. Did you divide words correctly?

Additional Writing Opportunities

Choose one of the following topics and write a response of one paragraph.

1. Alexander McCall Smith wrote the following in his book *The Full Cupboard of Life*:

   "Mr. J.L.B. Matekoni was not only the best mechanic in Botswana, but he was one of the kindest and most gracious of men. Mr. J.L.B. Matekoni would do anything for anyone who needed help and, in a world of increasing dishonesty, he still practiced the old Botswana morality. He was a good man, which when all is said and done, is the finest thing you can say about any man. He was a good man."

   What is a good man or woman? Give an example of a good person. It can be a person you know, a person in the news, or a character in a book. How does this person's goodness affect you?

2. There is an expression in English: "He would give me the shirt off his back." This means that the person is kind and generous. Write about a person who "would give you the shirt off his (or her) back." How do you know this person? How do you know that he or she is kind and generous?

3. How do children learn to do the right thing in life? Do they learn this from their parents, from religious leaders, from teachers, or from other children? Think of your own life and explain how you learned your values.

4. INTERNET RESEARCH: Aesop, La Fontaine, and Tolstoy wrote fables. Search the Internet for one of these writers and find out why he wrote this kind of story. When and where did he live? What was society like at the time? Write a brief report on what you find.

 Journal Writing

In your journal, write a response to the following questions. Don't worry about your mistakes. Try to write half a page.

Think about the people you know. Who is a happy person? What makes this person happy?

8 VIOLENT VIDEO GAMES

WRITING AN OPINION PARAGRAPH

In this unit you will practice:
- expressing opinions and giving reasons
- using gerunds and infinitives
- using expressions of opinion
- editing for sentence fragments with *because*

 Thinking About the Topic

Look at the pictures and think about the questions. Discuss your answers in small groups.

Why are video games so popular? Do you enjoy playing video games? Which games do you play? Where do you play them? If you don't play video games, explain why not.

II ▶ Reading for Writing

The computer is a big part of almost everyone's life. Adults, young adults, and children spend hour after hour in front of computer screens every day. Much of this time, people are playing computer games. The writer of this article discusses one kind of game: violent video games.

VIOLENT VIDEO GAMES: CAUSE FOR CONCERN

Entertainment companies make more money from the sale of video games than from the sale of movies. This is because young people all over the world spend a lot of time playing video games, and many of them are violent video games. Many parents, teachers, and psychologists are
5 very concerned about the effects of these games on the players. Some games encourage violent behavior against other people such as women, police officers, and people with different political views.

Some people believe that violent video games may be very harmful because they are interactive. That means, the player takes part in the
10 action of the game. The player becomes an aggressor, the person who plans the attack and causes the violence. Many people worry that children will become too aggressive in real life. They believe that children will learn to find solutions to problems only through violence.

Some researchers are studying the effects of violent video games. One
15 study included 210 college students. Some of the students played violent video games like "Grand Theft Auto" and some played non-violent video games like "Myst." The study showed that students who played more violent video games showed more aggressive behavior.

In Washington State, there is a law against selling violent video games
20 to young people under age 17. Storeowners who sell these games to children must pay a fine of $500. Other states are considering such a law. Many people want to completely ban, or forbid, the sale of these violent games.

We need to understand the possible dangers of violent video games.
25 The question is: What can we do about this serious problem?

General Understanding

1. Identifying the Issues

Read these questions. Put a check (✓) next to the correct answer(s). There may be more than one answer for each question. Discuss your answers with a partner.

1. Why are some people against violent video games?

_____ a. Some games encourage violence against police officers.

_____ b. Violent video games make college students more aggressive.

_____ c. All aggressive people like video games.

2. What are people doing now about the problem of violent video games?

_____ a. Researchers are studying the effects of violent video games.

_____ b. In Washington State, only people over age 17 can buy violent video games.

_____ c. Some states ban violent video games.

2. Drawing Conclusions

Work with a partner. Which statements support, or agree with, the ideas in the reading? Put a check (✓) next to them.

_____ 1. All the worry about video games is silly because video games are unimportant.

_____ 2. Young people may think aggressive behavior is acceptable.

_____ 3. People get used to seeing or hearing a lot of violence. They stop thinking that violence is a bad thing.

_____ 4. Violent video games let people express their aggression in play instead of in real life.

_____ 5. Violent video games are exciting; everything goes fast.

_____ 6. Boys who treat women badly in video games will not grow up to be good husbands and fathers.

3. Your Turn

Choose one of the statements in exercise 2 on page 87, and think about why you agree or disagree with it. Write your answer. Then discuss your answers in small groups.

_____

_____

_____

_____

4. Open for Discussion

Think about the following statements. Do you agree or disagree? Why? Discuss your opinions in small groups.

1. Girls like video games as much as boys do.

2. The games of our childhood affect our adult behavior.

3. Sometimes in life it is important to be aggressive.

4. A person over age 17 can make better choices than a young child.

After your discussions, choose one statement and write your opinion. Remember to write complete sentences.

_____

_____

_____

_____

_____

_____

III Writing Focus

A. Language for Writing: Gerunds and Infinitives

Study the sentences below. Pay attention to the verbs. Which verb goes with an infinitive (to + base form)? Which verb goes with a gerund (-ing form)? Which verb can go with both an infinitive and a gerund?

I want to play video games. I like to play video games.
I enjoy playing video games. I like playing video games.

This chart lists some verbs and expressions according to the forms they go with and the patterns they follow.

1. Verb + Infinitive

decide   promise
learn   refuse
need   want
plan

I **refuse to play** video games.

2. Verb + Gerund

avoid   imagine
enjoy   spend time
dislike*

I **spend time playing** video games.

3. Verb + Infinitive or Gerund

begin   love
continue   prefer
hate   start
like

I **love to play** video games.
I **love playing** video games.

4. Expressions + Preposition + Gerund

be in favor of   do something without
be against   see a difference between
be opposed to   see a relationship between

I **am against playing** video games.

* *Like* takes both the infinitive and gerund. However, *dislike* takes only the gerund.

1. Completing Paragraphs

Work with a partner. Fill in the blanks in the paragraphs with the correct forms of the verbs in parentheses. Use the chart on page 89 as a guide.

A Video Game Player's Point of View

1. Violent video games are fun. I like _to play/playing_ *(play)* them.

   I spend a lot of time every day _____ *(play)* different games like

   Doom, Wolfenstein 3D, Mortal Kombat, and Devil M. I like _____

   (kill) demons on Devil M, but that doesn't mean I want _____

   (kill) real human beings. Obviously, I see the difference between

   _____ *(imagine)* a fight and _____ *(live)* in the real world.

2. I enjoy _____ *(play)* violent video games. They help me express

   my anger without _____ *(hurt)* anybody. That is one reason why

   I am in favor of _____ *(let)* teenagers play violent video games.

   They can learn _____ *(express)* their feelings in the games and

   avoid _____ *(harm)* others.

3. I don't believe there is any relationship between _____ *(play)*

   violent video games and _____ *(become)* a criminal. I say this

   because Japanese teenagers prefer _____ *(play)* more violent

   games than American teenagers do, and there is much less crime in Japan.

2. Using Gerunds and Infinitives

Write a short paragraph about what you like to do in your free time. Use the structures you learned in this section. Share your paragraph with a partner.

_____

_____

_____

_____

B. Words and Ideas: Expressions of Opinion

You can use the following expressions to give your point of view, or opinion, about a question for discussion.

"YES"	"NO"
I am for	I am against
I am in favor of	I am opposed to
I agree with	I disagree with

I am for banning violent video games.
I am against banning violent video games.

These expressions all end in prepositions. They take gerunds because prepositions take gerunds.

After you express an opinion, you need to explain your reasons. One way to give your reasons is with *because*.

Read the following question and the opinions about it.

Should we **ban** the sale of violent video games?

Opinion A: (Yes) **I am for banning** the sale of violent video games **because** there is already too much real violence in our society. The violent play in the games can lead to aggression in real life. We should do everything possible to avoid this situation.

Opinion B: (No) **I am against banning** the sale of violent video games **because** people usually do not like to hear the word "No." It makes them find illegal ways to do what they want. Banning the sale of violent video games will cause a lot of crime.

Do you think we should ban the sale of violent video games? Write your opinion and give your reasons.

_____

_____

_____

_____

1. Stating Opinions and Giving Reasons

*Read the questions below. First decide on your point of view, "Yes" or "No." Use the expressions you learned and the words in **bold** print to express your opinions. Then give your reasons. Share your answers with a partner.*

1. Should we **protect** children under age 17 from the dangers of violent video games?

_____

_____

_____

_____

2. Should we **let** the government, rather than parents, decide what is right and what is wrong for children?

_____

_____

_____

_____

2. Categorizing Your Opinions

Review your ideas on page 91 and in exercise 1, above. Then look at the chart below. Which ideas support Opinion A? Which ones support Opinion B? Write your ideas in the appropriate boxes.

Opinion A: We should allow the sale of violent video games to children under age 17.	Opinion B: We should not allow the sale of violent video games to children under age 17.

YOUR TASK

Should we allow the sale of violent video games to children under age 17? Write an opinion paragraph that explains your answer to this question. Give at least three reasons for your opinion.

ALTERNATIVE TASK: **Should we ban songs with violent and offensive language? Write an opinion paragraph that explains your answer to this question. Give at least three reasons for your opinion.**

Step 1:   Getting Ideas

Choose the question you want to answer. Then decide on your point of view: Is your answer "Yes" or "No"? Put a check (✓) next to your answer below, and circle the opinion you want to write about.

TASK:

_____ Yes: I am **in favor of** allowing the sale of violent video games to children under age 17.

_____ No: I am **opposed to** allowing the sale of violent video games to children under age 17.

ALTERNATIVE TASK:

_____ Yes: I am **for** banning violent songs.

_____ No: I am **against** banning violent songs.

Write notes to support your opinion. Be sure to review the ideas you read and discussed in this unit.

_____

_____

_____

_____

_____

_____

Step 2: Organizing the Opinion Paragraph

Read the following paragraph. It expresses one student's opinion about children and TV. Pay attention to the key parts of the paragraph.

Topic Sentence (Opinion) ⟶ I am against letting children spend too much time watching TV.

Reason 1 ⟶ First of all, too much TV is not good for their health. Children become overweight because they spend more time watching TV than exercising.

Reason 2 ⟶ Their eyesight also gets worse. With bad eyesight, it is hard to read and do homework. As a result, children lose interest in school.

Reason 3 ⟶ Watching TV for hours also affects children socially. They don't learn how to get along with other people because they don't have to talk to anyone. This hurts their social development. TV is often educational

Concluding Sentence ⟶ and fun, but too much TV causes problems. That is why I think we should limit children's TV time.

Step 3: Writing a Concluding Sentence

A concluding sentence repeats the main idea of the topic sentence, but the writer uses different words.

Now write your paragraph. Be sure to include all the key parts.

Step 4: Revising

Work with a partner. Read each other's paragraphs, and write comments in the margin. Use the checklist below. Don't worry about grammar errors.

> ## CHECKLIST FOR REVISING
>
> **1. Does the writer express a clear opinion in the topic sentence?**
>
> **2. Does the writer give reasons?**
>
> **3. Does the concluding sentence have the same message as the topic sentence? Does it use different words?**

Review your writing. Do you want to change any part of the paragraph to make it clearer? Do you want to add any ideas?

Step 5: Editing—Sentence Fragments

Fragments are pieces of sentences. They cannot stand alone.

Fragments (Incorrect)
Because they contain bad language.
We should ban violent songs. Because they contain bad language.

Correct
We should ban violent songs because they contain bad language.
Because* they contain bad language, we should ban violent songs.

*Note: When *Because* comes at the beginning of the sentence, use a comma to separate the two parts of the sentence.

Circle the fragments in the paragraphs below and rewrite the sentences correctly in your notebooks.

1. I am for banning violent songs. Many people do not like this music. (Because they think it is offensive.) Because the heroes of these songs are often criminals. This music brings more violence to our society. Sadly, many singers of these songs are very popular. Because some listeners think they are cool. We should protect young people from the bad influence of this music. That is why I think we should ban it.

2. I am against banning violent songs. Because people have the right to choose. Many people listen to these songs. Because they like to hear bad language. They also like this music. Because it sends the message that bad language is okay. I don't enjoy listening to this music. However, I don't want to ban it. Because it's wrong to make a law that bans ideas you don't like.

Read each sentence of your paragraph carefully. Edit any grammar errors you find. Use the checklist below.

CHECKLIST FOR EDITING:

1. Did you use gerunds and infinitives correctly?

2. Did you use correct expressions to state your opinion?

3. Did you avoid using sentence fragments?

IV Additional Writing Opportunities

Choose one of the following topics and write a response of one paragraph.

1. Do our childhood games affect our adult behavior? Write about the games you played as a child. Did you play alone, or did you play with other children? Did you play individual sports (like swimming and tennis) or did you play team sports (like volleyball and soccer)? Did these experiences affect the person you are today?

2. Should parents let their children choose the books they want to read, the movies they want to see, and the games they want to play? What do you think? Why?

3. How can we teach our children to live in peace with people from many different cultures and ethnic groups? What important ideas should we teach them?

4. "Video games are a total waste of time. Children should spend more time playing sports and participating in other social activities." Do you agree or disagree with this statement? Explain your answer.

5. INTERNET RESEARCH: Do violent sports lead to violent behavior? Search the Internet for information about sports like ice hockey, boxing, wrestling, American football, rugby, and soccer. What do experts say? Does the violence in these sports affect the behavior of people who watch them? Write a brief report on what you find.

 ## Journal Writing

In your journal, write a response to the following questions. Don't worry about mistakes. Try to write half a page.

What do you do in your personal "quiet time"? How does this activity help you live with the stress of everyday life?

Answer Key

UNIT 1
WHAT'S IN A NAME?

II. Reading for Writing
General Understanding
1. Comparing Cultures (page 3)

United States culture

2. a few days after birth
3. yes

Bengali culture

1. the grandparents of the parents/great-grandparents
2. a long time, even years, after birth
3. no

2. Explaining Reasons (page 3)

Answers will vary. Some examples are:

1. Ashima and Ashoke have a problem because they don't have a name for their baby.
2. The parents cannot name this baby because they don't have the grandmother's letter with the name.
3. The baby cannot leave the hospital because he doesn't have a name.
4. Bengali parents cannot name a child after another family member because each name is special.

III. Writing Focus
A. Language for Writing
1. Working on the Simple Present Tense (page 6)

2. A baby cries for many reasons.
3. Ashoke doesn't/does not have an English name.
4. Ashima isn't/is not comfortable with American naming traditions.
5. Who pays for a name change?

2. Completing a Paragraph (page 6)

2. gives
3. doesn't stop/does not stop
4. tells
5. are
6. have
7. are
8. comes
9. means
10. explain

B. Words and Ideas
2. Choosing Adjectives (page 8)

2. cheerful
3. confident
4. athletic
5. attractive
6. hardworking
7. shy
8. honest

C. YOUR TASK
Step 5: Editing—Capital Letters (page 11)

In the United States, there are many last names from other languages. There are Polish names like Polanski, Chinese names like Woo, Italian names like Pacino, Korean names like Park, and Spanish names like Lopez. Some names can be written in Greek or Arabic letters. A family name such as Pavlova means "a female member of the Pavlov family" in Russian. All these names tell the story of America.

UNIT 2
GIVING ADVICE

II. Reading for Writing
General Understanding
1. True or False? (page 15)

1. T
2. F
3. F
4. F

2. Explaining Reasons (page 15)

1. a, b, d
2. a, c, d

III. Writing Focus
A. Language for Writing
1. Correcting Statements with *Should* (page 17)

2. Should we give our money to homeless people?
3. I should tell the police about the problem.
4. He shouldn't give his money to homeless people.
5. What should we do?

2. Completing Sentences with *Should* and *Shouldn't* (page 18)

2. should build
3. shouldn't have
4. should raise

5. shouldn't live

6. should create

7. Shouldn't we care

8. should have

B. Words and Ideas

1. Recognizing Meanings (page 19)

2. interested

3. depressed

4. frightened

5. bored

6. thrilled

2. Recognizing Word Forms (page 20)

2. boring

3. interesting

4. surprised

5. frightening

6. thrilling

7. depressed

C. YOUR TASK

Step 5: Editing—Fixing Comma Splices (page 23)

Dear Mayor Clark:

I agree with you, Mr. Mayor. I am also very surprised at the way people behave in the subway. Young men rush to get the seats. They don't think about others. Elderly people are tired. They need a rest during the long train ride. Pregnant women also need seats. My advice is to have an official card showing that a person is over 65, or disabled, or pregnant. That's a good way to stop all the arguments. People will have to get up from their seats. Good manners will become the law.

Maggie Carlton

UNIT 3

CREATING GARDENS—BUILDING COMMUNITY

II. Reading for Writing

General Understanding

1. Explaining Goals and Results (page 27)

Answers will vary. Some examples are:

1. The neighbors are working together because they want to create a community garden.

2. In the past, the area was full of garbage, rusty nails, rocks, and broken glass. Now there are many plants, flowers, fruits, and vegetables.

2. Focusing on the Details (page 27)

Answers will vary. Some examples are:

Environmental (Gardening) Activities: The gardeners plant flowers, fruits, and vegetables; they water the plants; they watch the garden grow; they harvest fruits and vegetables.

Educational Activities: Experts give advice about gardening; students study the natural environment; people discuss the movies they see.

Social and Cultural Activities: People work in the garden together; musicians play music; people sit quietly and read; people watch movies together.

III. Writing Focus

A. Language for Writing

1. Completing a Letter (page 30)

2. will learn

3. will understand

4. will save

5. won't have to/will not have to

6. will be

7. will breathe

8. will become

9. will come

10. will visit

B. Words and Ideas

1. Completing Sentences (page 32)

2. quietly

3. hard

4. happily

5. regularly

6. patiently

7. beautifully

8. well

C. YOUR TASK

Step 5: Editing—More Rules on Capitalization (page 35)

August 14, 2006

Dear Mayor Black,

I am writing to ask for your help. We want to organize a Halloween parade for the children in our neighborhood. The teachers and parents from Bayside High School will help us. We want to march from Maple Street to Sixth Avenue on Friday, October 31. Please help us get permission for this parade.

Thank you for your help.

Sincerely,
Patricia Kopernic
Patricia Kopernic,
President, Bayside Beautification Group

UNIT 4
WORK

II. Reading for Writing
General Understanding
1. True or False? (page 39)
1. F
2. F
3. T
4. F

2. Explaining Reasons (page 39)
2. d
3. b
4. a

III. Writing Focus
A. Language for Writing
Using the Simple Past (page 42)
2. was
3. didn't have/did not have
4. were
5. went
6. became
7. began
8. learned
9. decided
10. were
11. helped
12. asked
13. traveled
14. were
15. didn't want/did not want
16. wasn't/was not
17. didn't stop/did not stop
18. knew

B. Words and Ideas
Using Negative Prefixes (page 44)
unemployed	inhumane
unhappy	illegal
unhealthy	impossible
dishonest	unskilled

2. impossible
3. unhealthy
4. dishonest
5. unemployed
6. unhappy
7. Unskilled
8. illegal

C. YOUR TASK
Step 5: Editing—Punctuation Rules
(page 47)

My Job
This summer I had the coolest job. I worked for Juno Enterprises X on 57th St. and 6th Ave. It's one of the largest entertainment companies in the U.S. Lots of singers, actors, and musicians came into the office every day. Sometimes I even saw big TV stars! I made photocopies X and delivered packages. Ms. Young X was my manager. She made me wear a boring suit every day, but I didn't mind. That's the way you dress for success! Why did I work so hard? I want to be a manager in a company like this someday. Who knows?

UNIT 5
FREE AS A BIRD

II. Reading for Writing
General Understanding
1. Main Idea (page 51)
1. a, c
2. b, c
Answers will vary. Some examples are:
The birds are small and weak, but they are free and happy.
The lion is the king of the animal world, but he is imprisoned and sad.

2. Agree or Disagree? (page 51)
Answers will vary. Some examples are:
1. A/D—Zola is sad to see the lions, but he is happy to see the birds.
2. A
3. A/D—The birds are happy because they are free. It's possible that the birds are free because they are unimportant. Nobody goes to a zoo to see sparrows, but people do go to see a lion.
4. A
5. D—Dreams are very important for the weak and powerless. Dreams help these people see outside their world. But everyone needs to dream.

III. Writing Focus
A. Language for Writing
1. Choosing the Correct Verb Tense (page 53)
2. went
3. saw
4. will help
5. married
6. speaks

2. Completing Paragraphs (page 54)
2. is
3. accepts
4. will continue
5. makes/will make
6. come
7. spend
8. visited

B. Words and Ideas
1. Completing Sentences (page 55)
1. in
2. in, with
3. about, of
4. without, at
5. in, in

C. YOUR TASK
Step 5: Editing—*Its* and *It's* (page 59)
2. It's not fair to kill animals that don't have homes.
3. An animal gives you all its love.
4. It's the story of a man who learns about love by taking care of birds.
5. Its fur is very soft.
6. It's important to understand our relationship with nature.

UNIT 6
EDUCATION: GRAPHING PROGRESS
II. Reading for Writing
What Is a Graph? (page 62)
1. years
2. literacy rates in percents
3. 3 groups or categories, 3 lines
4. literacy rates for men, women, and total (men + women)

General Understanding
1. Reading the Statistics: True or False? (page 63)
1. T
2. F
3. F
4. F (Literacy went up in both periods.)
5. T (The average difference is becoming smaller, but that does not mean that the difference is becoming smaller in every country in the world.)

2. Thinking about Reasons (page 63)
1, 3, 4

III. Writing Focus
A. Language for Writing
Using *More…than, Fewer…than, Less…than* (page 66)
2. fewer … than
3. more … than
4. more … than
5. more … than
6. more … than … less

B. Words and Ideas
1. Matching Words and Meanings (page 66)
2. c
3. d
4. e
5. a

2. Completing a Paragraph (page 67)
2. percent
3. total
4. increase
5. decrease

3. Discussing Statistics (page 68)
1. The graph is about the number of American men who had college degrees in the year 2000.
2. The x-axis shows the ages of the men in

2000. The y-axis shows the percent of each group with B.A. degrees.

3. More American men are getting college degrees these days than in the past. More younger men have college degrees than senior men do.

4. *Example answer:* Today, there are many different kinds of colleges, more scholarships, and more opportunities for non-traditional students in their 20's or 30's to go back to school. With the growth in technology, there is less demand for people to do physical work than for people with good reading, writing, and computer skills. More people find it necessary to go back to college.

5. *Example answer:* There are probably fewer senior women than senior men with B.A. degrees. The percentages of younger women with B.A. degrees are probably similar to the percentages of younger men with B.A. degrees.

C. YOUR TASK
Step 5: Editing—Subject–Verb Agreement (page 71)
2. people get
3. Education gives
4. ✓ (correct)
5. men and women…lead
6. lives…need

UNIT 7
TOLSTOY'S FABLES
II. Reading for Writing
General Understanding
1. Summarizing the Story (page 75)
1. b
2. e
3. d
4. c
5. a

2. Thinking About the Moral of the Story (page 75)
Answers may vary.
1, 4, 5
(2 is incorrect because both rich and poor people can be happy. Tolstoy's message to all people is that the key to happiness is living a simple life.)

III. Writing Focus
A. Language for Writing
1. Correcting Sentences (page 77)
2. The wise man <u>wants to help</u> the king.
3. The king's son <u>wants his father to feel</u> better.
4. The poor man <u>would like to help</u> the king.
5. The king's bodyguards <u>ask the happy man to give</u> them his shirt.

2. Writing Sentences (page 78)
2. The wise men would like the king to be happy.
3. The wise men would like to find a happy man.
4. The rich man would like to be healthy.
5. The healthy man wants to have more money.
6. The king's son asks the poor man to give him his shirt.
7. The king's son would like to give the poor man a lot of money.
8. The poor man would like to help the king.

B. Words and Ideas
Choosing Adjective and Noun Forms (page 80)
2. sick
3. happy
4. illness
5. wealthy
6. ill
7. rich
8. health
9. importance
10. happy

C. YOUR TASK
Step 5: Editing—Word Division (page 83)
3. king-dom
4. im-por-tant
5. hap-pi-ness
6. eve-ry-thing
7. health
8. ✓ (correct)
9. emp-ty

UNIT 8
VIOLENT VIDEO GAMES

II. Reading for Writing
General Understanding
1. Identifying the Issues (page 87)

1. a, b
2. a, b

2. Drawing Conclusions (page 87)

2, 3, 6

III. Writing Focus
A. Language for Writing
1. Completing Paragraphs (page 90)

2. playing
3. to kill/killing
4. to kill
5. imagining
6. living
7. playing
8. hurting
9. letting
10. to express
11. harming
12. playing
13. becoming
14. to play/playing

B. Words and Ideas
1. Stating Opinions and Giving Reasons (page 92)

1. I am in favor of protecting children.../I am for protecting children.../I agree with protecting children...
OR
I am against protecting.../I am opposed to protecting.../I disagree with protecting...

2. I am in favor of letting the government.../I am for letting the government.../I agree with letting the government...
OR
I am against letting the government.../I am opposed to letting the government.../I disagree with letting the government...

C. YOUR TASK
Step 5: Editing—Sentence Fragments (page 95)

1. Many people do not like this music because they think it is offensive. Because the heroes of these songs are often criminals, this music brings more violence to our society. Sadly, many singers of these songs are very popular because some listeners think they are cool.

2. I am against banning violent songs because people have the right to choose. Many people listen to these songs because they like to hear bad language. They also like this music because it sends the message that bad language is okay. However, I don't want to ban it because it's wrong to make a law that bans ideas you don't like.